OXFORD
SLAVONIC PAPERS

Edited by

ROBERT AUTY   J. L. I. FENNELL

and

I. P. FOOTE

General Editor

NEW SERIES

VOLUME IX

CLARENDON PRESS · OXFORD

1976

Oxford University Press, Ely House, London W.1

OXFORD LONDON GLASGOW NEW YORK
TORONTO MELBOURNE WELLINGTON CAPE TOWN
IBADAN NAIROBI DAR ES SALAAM LUSAKA ADDIS ABABA
KUALA LUMPUR SINGAPORE JAKARTA HONG KONG TOKYO
DELHI BOMBAY CALCUTTA MADRAS KARACHI

ISBN 0 19 815650 2

© Oxford University Press 1976

*Text set in 10/11 pt. Monotype Baskerville, printed by letterpress, and bound in Great Britain at
The Pitman Press, Bath*

8/29/79

THE editorial policy of the New Series of *Oxford Slavonic Papers* in general follows that of the original series, thirteen volumes of which appeared between the years 1950 and 1967 under the editorship of Professor S. Konovalov (volumes 11 to 13 edited jointly with Mr. J. S. G. Simmons, who also acted as General Editor of the New Series, volumes 1 to 4). It is devoted to the publication of original contributions and documents relating to the languages, literatures, culture, and history of Russia and the other Slavonic countries, and appears annually towards the end of the year. Reviews of individual books are not normally included, but bibliographical and review articles are published from time to time.

The British System of Cyrillic transliteration (British Standard 2979: 1958) has been adopted, omitting diacritics and using -y to express -й, -ий, -ій, and -ый at the end of proper names, e.g. Sergey, Dostoevsky, Bely, Grozny. For philological work the International System (ISO R/9) is used.

ROBERT AUTY
J. L. I. FENNELL
I. P. FOOTE

The Queen's College, Oxford

CONTENTS

Medieval Russian Culture in the Writings of D. S. Likhachev

By DIMITRI OBOLENSKY

DMITRY Sergeevich Likhachev's seventieth birthday, which falls on 28 November of this year, provides an opportunity to reflect on the significance of the work accomplished so far by this eminent medievalist. His entire life has been intimately associated with his native city, St. Petersburg–Petrograd–Leningrad. As a student in its University (1923–8) he worked simultaneously in two sections—the Romance–Germanic and the Slavo–Russian—of the department of linguistics and literature. In the first section he specialized in English literature, writing a thesis on 'Shakespeare in Russia in the Eighteenth Century'. In the second section he worked on some unpublished works of the poet Nekrasov and, under the supervision of the well-known literary historian and palaeographer D. I. Abramovich, studied medieval Russian literature.

In 1938, ten years after his graduation, Likhachev became associated with the Institute of Russian Literature of the Academy of Sciences of the USSR (*Pushkinskii dom*). This affiliation was to play a central role in his scholarly life. In 1954 he was appointed director of its medieval Russian literature section, a position he still holds. In this capacity he has done much to build the *Sektor drevnerusskoi literatury* of *Pushkinskii dom* into the leading world centre for the study of early Russian literature. Its journal, *Trudy Otdela drevnerusskoi literatury*, enjoys a unique reputation and authority in this field.

He obtained his doctorate in 1947, and in 1951 was appointed professor in the University of Leningrad. In 1953 he became a Corresponding Member of the Soviet Academy of Sciences, and in November 1970 was elected to full membership of the Academy. In 1967 he came to Britain where, on 16 February, he was awarded by Oxford University the honorary degree of Doctor of Letters. In 1976 he was elected a Corresponding Fellow of the British Academy.

An important, though less widely known, aspect of Likhachev's public activity has been his contribution to the preservation of historic monuments in his native country. By a fortunate coincidence, some of his early works on medieval Russian culture appeared in the aftermath of the Second World War, when many of these monuments lay in ruins after the German occupation. There is no doubt that his writings (notably his book on medieval Novgorod, published in 1945) did much to publicize the need to carry out a widespread programme of restoration. Later, particularly in the 'fifties and 'sixties, he frequently published articles in the Soviet press, drawing attention to the danger of allowing ancient monuments to go to ruin through ignorance or neglect. In this respect his educative role has been considerable.

The wide range of subjects covered by Likhachev's writings[1] makes any classification of them difficult. Nevertheless, three major themes are detectable in his published works: (1) medieval Russian chronicles; (2) the *Slovo o polku Igoreve*; (3) the literary and cultural history of medieval Russia. The aim of this article is to assess his contribution to each of these subjects.

I

Likhachev's life-long interest in Russian chronicles found an outlet in the late 1930s, when he undertook a study of the writings of A. A. Shakhmatov (1864–1920), the foremost authority in this field. From Shakhmatov he acquired a sophisticated and well-tried textological technique, the purpose of which was to determine the relationship between the extant chronicle texts, to reconstruct the prototypes from which they were derived, and to discover the genetic processes by which the extant texts acquired their present form. These processes, Shakhmatov argued, were often connected with the political views of the successive chronicle compilers, or of their patrons. The acceptance of his master's methodology gave Likhachev a knowledge, unrivalled among his contemporaries, of the history of Russian chronicle writing; and an understanding—heightened by his own abiding interest in the history of ideas—of how closely the process of writing and revision of chronicles was linked to the political and social history of medieval Russia. In one respect he was able to improve on Shakhmatov's 'historical' method: for he approached his subject not just as a historian or a philologist, but as a student of literature as well; and in so doing he identified and described not only the ideology but also the literary style of a number of medieval chroniclers. This historico-literary approach has advanced our understanding of their aesthetic standards and literary achievements.

Likhachev's *début* in the historiographical field was a study of the twelfth-century chronicle text of Novgorod. His first work of synthesis on this subject was a general study of the cultural and historical significance of Russian chronicles (*Russkie letopisi i ikh kul'turno-istoricheskoe znachenie*, M.–L., 1947). Its opening chapters are devoted to the masterpiece of medieval Russian historiography, the *Povest' vremennykh let*, or Russian Primary Chronicle. In seeking to determine the history of its text he naturally started from the 'genealogical tree' proposed by Shakhmatov. This involves the acceptance of a complex and hypothetical pedigree: an early version of the Chronicle which goes back to the reign of Prince Yaroslav of Kiev (1019–54); a second, expanded version, compiled about 1073 in the Kiev Monastery of the Caves; a third compilation, further enlarged, carried out in the same monastery between 1093 and 1095; and a fourth text, the *Povest' vremennykh let*, written probably in 1113 by the monk Nestor of the Monastery of the Caves: this version, distinguished by the addition of a large amount of material of

[1] In a bibliography published in 1966 his published works numbered over three hundred. See *Dmitry Sergeevich Likhachev* (M., 1966) (*Materialy k biobibliografii uchenykh SSSR, seriya literatury i yazyka*, vyp. 7). See also V. Adrianova-Peretts, L. Dmitriev and Ya. Lur'e, 'Dmitry Sergeevich Likhachev', *Russkaya literatura*, 1966 no. 3, pp. 233–40.

Byzantine origin and by its author's sophisticated view of Russia's past in relation to the surrounding world, is already close to the extant one; two further versions, however, (compiled in 1116 and 1118–19) were postulated by Shakhmatov before the Primary Chronicle acquired its present form.

Except in one respect, Likhachev has in the main accepted this stemma. It is only Shakhmatov's hypothetical earliest text, dated to 1037–9, that he rejects, substituting for it an equally hypothetical 'Tale of the Spread of Christianity in Russia', which he reconstructs from six passages embedded in the extant version of the Primary Chronicle: they relate to the baptism and death of Princess Ol'ga (s.a. 955, 969), the martyrdom of two Varangian Christians in Kiev (s.a. 983), the original core of the story of Vladimir's conversion (s.a. 986, 987, 988), the murder of Boris and Gleb (s.a. 1015), and the panegyric of Prince Yaroslav (s.a. 1037). He believes that this lengthy account of Russia's conversion, which he dates to the reign of Yaroslav, was the archetype from which the existing text of the Primary Chronicle ultimately descended.

In *Russkie letopisi*, and in some of his later works, Likhachev has argued that the 'Tale of the Spread of Christianity in Russia' was the Primary Chronicle's distant ancestor. He has also tried to determine its author's literary manner, compositional technique, and outlook. The ideological parallels he finds between this work and Hilarion's *Slovo o zakone i blagodati* are convincing enough; and although, in this writer's opinion, he unjustly accuses Hilarion of harbouring anti-Byzantine sentiments, he is surely right in detecting in these two mid-eleventh-century works the earliest literary instances of Russian national self-determination.

It is generally believed that the material of the earliest layers of the Primary Chronicle is in part derived from oral tradition; Likhachev has shown that successive compilers of the Primary Chronicle between 1064 and 1106 drew heavily on the oral accounts of Vyshata and Yan, father and son, who were members of a distinguished Kievan and Novgorodian family. Other oral sources, not mentioned by Likhachev in this work, may have been of more specifically Scandinavian origin. In a remarkable, and unjustly neglected book, *Die Varägersage als Quelle der altrussischen Chronik* (Aarhus–Leipzig, 1934), A. Stender-Petersen argued that some of the chronicle stories, narrating the adventures and military exploits of the early rulers of Kiev, are fragments of a saga tradition, brought to Russia by Scandinavian Varangians who had served in the Byzantine armed forces in the Mediterranean area. Not all features of Stender-Petersen's thesis may be equally convincing; but it is surely time that it be brought more widely to bear on the problem of the origins of the Primary Chronicle.[2]

One of the most impressive sections of *Russkie letopisi* (pp. 100–44) deals with the style and structure of the Primary Chronicle. Likhachev's brief but superb analysis of the use of direct speech and dialogue takes us out of the occasionally arid world of textology into that of vivid portrayal, dramatic suspense and racy humour: it is as though the sturdy but somewhat bare

---

[2] In a later work, *Razvitie russkoi literatury X–XVII vekov* (L., 1973), 18–19, Likhachev does refer to the 'Varangian traditions' in the Primary Chronicle, and to Stender-Petersen's book.

genealogical tree sketched by Shakhmatov had acquired leaves and flowers, painted in by a master of literary characterization.

The remaining part of *Russkie letopisi* discusses post-Kievan chronicle writing: the chronicles of Novgorod, compiled in the twelfth and the fifteenth centuries, two crucial periods of the city's cultural history; the decline of historiography after the Mongol invasion; the provincialization of chronicle writing on the periphery of the land; and the attempts, in the late Middle Ages, by Muscovite ideologues to centralize and monopolize chronicle writing in an effort to claim for Muscovy the historical inheritance of Kievan Russia.

It is hardly surprising that the most vivid and memorable passages in *Russkie letopisi* are devoted to the Primary Chronicle. For, alongside the *Slovo o polku Igoreve*, this is the work of medieval Russian literature that has most inspired Likhachev. It is not hard to see why. To a medievalist experienced in questions of textology, interested in the history of ideas, and possessing in addition a keen sense of aesthetic values, the appeal of the Primary Chronicle is irresistible. Its style combines the solemn language of religious instruction, a lyricism derived partly from the Christian liturgy and partly from folk poetry, the art of the story-teller, the use of dramatic dialogue and of the pungent and humorous aphorism. Its authors show themselves capable of reflecting on the meaning and purpose of history. They also, and none more than Nestor, reveal a moral sense outraged by cruelty and injustice, a recognition of the social benefits conferred by the Christian religion, a high regard for education, and an awareness that the Russian people, through their recent acceptance of Christianity, have become members of the larger family of mankind. No wonder that in his later writings Likhachev frequently returned to the Primary Chronicle. In 1950 he published a critical edition of its text (*Povest' vremennykh let*, 2 vols.), accompanied by a modern Russian translation, a detailed historical and literary introduction, and an ample commentary of great value. For every student of medieval Russia these two volumes have become a standard work.

II

Likhachev's interest in the *Slovo o polku Igoreve* became apparent in 1949 and 1950 when he published a series of studies on, and a critical edition of, this heroic poem. The edition appeared in a co-operative work, *Slovo o polku Igoreve*, edited by V. P. Adrianova-Peretts (M.–L., 1950), to which Likhachev contributed the greater part: a reconstruction of the text, an 'explanatory translation' into modern Russian, a historical and literary study of the poem, an account of the circumstances of its discovery in the early 1790s and its publication in 1800, and an extensive commentary. His editorial experience, knowledge of twelfth-century Russia, and aesthetic sensitivity are happily combined in this book. Though not all of his textual emendations have secured unqualified assent (in this and other respects his edition should be compared with that of Roman Jakobson), many of them are illuminating. The historical context is sketched with scholarship and artistry. Believing that the poem was written in 1187, he strives to show that it faithfully mirrors the ideals, culture, and preoccupations of Russian society in the closing decades of the 'Kievan' period: the ambitions, chivalrous or selfish, of its princes, the danger of military invasion by the pagan Polovtsy from the steppe, the declining role of Kiev, the former capital, and the continued emotional appeal, at least to patriotic Russians, of the concept of the 'Russian land', a common patrimony in terms of territory, language and religion. Patriotism, Likhachev believes, is the central message of the *Slovo*. Certainly its author expends much eloquence in urging the princes of Russia to unite in defence of Kiev, and in demonstrating that the victories of the pagans are the result of the disunity among the princes of the land. However, this patriotic and didactic theme has in the poem a counterpart. Igor' and his companions, who suffer defeat and captivity at the hands of the Polovtsy and whose foolhardy campaign, undertaken for personal glory, is from a national point of view a disaster, are yet, from another standpoint, held up for admiration: their courage and prowess on the field of battle and the tragic dignity of their defeat are designed to move and exalt the audience, in the true tradition of heroic poetry. These two themes, the heroic and the patriotic, are balanced and sometimes blended in the poem with great artistry. Perhaps too little attention, at least in recent times, has been devoted to the purely heroic component of the *Slovo*.

In the 1960s, Likhachev became involved in the controversy regarding the authenticity of the *Slovo*. This debate, which began in the first half of the nineteenth century and later subsided, flared up again after the publication in 1940 of André Mazon's book *Le Slovo d'Igor*, and in 1963 was imported from France to Russia by the Soviet medievalist A. A. Zimin.[3] Both Mazon and Zimin believe that the *Slovo* is a forgery, perpetrated in the late eighteenth century in imitation of the *Zadonshchina*, which is an epic work written in the late fourteenth or early fifteenth century to celebrate the Russian victory over the Tatars at the battle of Kulikovo in 1380. Since the discovery and publication of the *Zadonschina* in 1852 it has been obvious that the striking similarities between whole passages of the two works point to a direct connexion between them. Those who regard the *Slovo* as a medieval work are forced to conclude that it served as a model for the *Zadonshchina*. The 'sceptics' are equally compelled to reverse this relationship between the two works.

Inevitably, therefore, Likhachev was drawn into the intricate discussion about the relationship between the *Slovo* and the *Zadonshchina*. His contribution to the debate was made in three stages. At first he developed, as an argument against the sceptics, his concept of the 'poetics of imitation'.[4] By 'imitation' he means the endeavour to copy the style and imagery of the original work and to apply them in a different context to another subject, by mechanically borrowing ready-made phrases and formulae. This 'inertia

---

[3] For a brief survey of the history of this controversy see the chapter by J. Fennell, 'The Tale of Igor''s Campaign' in J. Fennell and A. Stokes, *Early Russian Literature* (1974), 191–206.
[4] The concept is defined by Likhachev in his *Poetika drevnerusskoi literatury*, 2 ed. (L., 1971), 203–31.

of imitation' leads to a simplified distortion of the original and to the appearance in the pastiche of stylistic incongruities. In his opinion, it is precisely
these signs of 'monotonous' and 'inconsistent' borrowing that are apparent
in the *Zadonshchina*, and not in the *Slovo*. If, he argues, one subtracts from
the *Zadonshchina* all the borrowings from the *Slovo*, nothing in the remainder
will resemble the *Slovo*. But if one excises from the *Slovo* all elements which
resemble the *Zadonshchina*, most of the remainder will be stylistically identical
with the excised passages of the *Slovo*. This textological argument acquires
added force if it is remembered that such imitations of works of the Kievan
period were typical of the late fourteenth and early fifteenth century, the
period when the *Zadonshchina* was written.

The second stage in Likhachev's investigation of the *Slovo–Zadonshchina*
relationship was marked by the appearance in 1966 of a book of major importance, '*Slovo o polku Igoreve*' *i pamyatniki Kulikovskogo tsikla*, of which he was the
joint editor. It is a co-operative work, whose 'organizer', in the words of its
preface, was V. P. Adrianova-Peretts, a scholar of great acumen who
helped Likhachev to find his vocation as a medievalist. Although it contains
no separate contribution by Likhachev (the chapter he wrote for it, 'The
imitative features of the *Zadonshchina*', was actually published earlier in
article form[5]), his influence is manifest in many sections. Two principal aims
are evident in this book of over 600 pages: to determine the time when the
Slovo was composed, and to discover its textological relationship to the works
concerned with the Battle of Kulikovo, especially of the *Zadonshchina*. One
of the main arguments used to date the *Slovo* is a linguistic one: is its language
compatible with a twelfth-century dating, or do its vocabulary and phraseology point to a later period in the development of the Russian language?
V. P. Adrianova-Peretts's detailed stylistic commentary on the *Slovo* provides
strong evidence to support the first alternative: she argues that the poem's
vocabulary, morphology, syntax, imagery, military terminology, and
lyrical diction, however 'peculiar' they may often appear, in fact wholly
correspond to our knowledge of the Russian literary language of the Kievan
period. The book's second aim is achieved by the most thorough study yet
undertaken of the six extant manuscripts of the *Zadonshchina*. Its authors set
out to refute the main textological argument of the 'sceptics': the argument
that the *Slovo* is closer to the later texts of the *Zadonshchina* than to the earliest
one. The dicussion is too complex to be summarized here. But whether or not
one accepts the view that this book is 'easily the weightiest attempt to con-
found the sceptics',[6] it will remain as a major landmark in the history of the
Slovo scholarship.

The third, most recent, stage in Likhachev's contribution to the problem
is marked by two articles in English, published in *Oxford Slavonic Papers*.
In the first, 'The Authenticity of the *Slovo o Polku Igoreve*: A Brief Survey of
the Arguments',[7] he takes up an argument originally put forward by Roman
Jakobson in 1952. It concerns the threefold relationship between the *Slovo*,

---

[5] 'Cherty podrazhatel'nosti "Zadonshchiny"', *Russkaya literatura*, 1964 no. 3, pp. 84–107.
[6] Fennell, op. cit. (n. 3), 195.
[7] *Oxford Slavonic Papers*, xiii (1967), 33–46.

the *Zadonshchina*, and the account of Igor' Svyatoslavich's 1185 campaign against the Polovtsy in the Hypatian Chronicle. This 'textological triangle' (the expression is Likhachev's) is used by him as an argument for the view that the *Zadonshchina* derives from the *Slovo*; for, were the opposite the case, it would follow that the author of the *Zadonshchina* knew the text of the Hypatian Chronicle and 'out of its innumerable accounts of Russian battles and campaigns, singled out that very account of the defeat of Igor Svyatoslavich which was later to provide the basis for the *Slovo o Polku Igoreve*'. Such a coincidence would be 'contrived and highly improbable' (p. 36).

In the second, more technical, article, 'Further Remarks on the Textological Triangle: *Slovo o polku Igoreve, Zadonshchina,* and the Hypatian Chronicle',[8] Likhachev explores the relationship between the three works—in response to John Fennell's attempt[9] to obliterate one side of the 'textological triangle' by denying any textual link between the *Zadonshchina* and the account of Igor''s campaign in the Hypatian Chronicle—and reiterates his earlier conclusion that the *Zadonshchina* derives from the *Slovo*. This view, which the present writer shares, is argued with Likhachev's customary lucidity and courtesy. In the first of his two English articles he wrote these words, alluding to the lengthy and often acrimonious *Slovo* controversy: 'Both sides should refrain from straying beyond the purely academic aspects of the question. One should not, for example, have recourse to "psychological" explanations of the attitudes of one's adversaries . . . and, finally, one should not try to impress by adducing the number of supporters of one's own point of view. These requirements are demanded not only by the ethics of academic dispute but also by simple logic.'[10]

III

A notable feature of Likhachev's work on Russian chronicles and on the *Slovo o polku Igoreve* is his ability to combine the technique of minute textual analysis with broader literary and historical perspectives, designed to test the validity of generalizations made from a comparative study of the relevant material. Thus the conclusions he reached by comparing the *Slovo* with the *Zadonshchina* enabled him to develop his concept of the literary imitation or pastiche. Similarly, his knowledge of medieval chronicles, as well as his use of Shakhmatov's methods, contributed to his book *Tekstologiya* (M.–L., 1962). Textology, he asserts, should be clearly distinguished from textual criticism: the two are related much as chemistry is to chemical analysis. The term 'textology' owes its existence to the Formalist critic B. V. Tomashevsky (1890–1957). In recent years, not least thanks to Likhachev, it has enjoyed a considerable vogue in Russian literary criticism. Textology aims to study

[8] *Oxford Slavonic Papers*, N.S., ii (1969), 106–15.
[9] 'The *Slovo o polku Igoreve*: the Textological Triangle', *Oxford Slavonic Papers*, N.S., i (1968), 126–37.
[10] 'The Authenticity of the *Slovo o Polku Igoreve*', *Oxford Slavonic Papers*, xiii (1967), 33.

the semantic and aesthetic properties of literary works, with particular reference to their successive redactions, and also the social and environmental conditions in which their authors and copyists lived and worked. The claims made for textology by Likhachev are high: it is not an applied discipline, he contends, but an 'independent science'.

Likhachev's interest in these broad conceptual structures, and in the theory of literature, has increased of late. It can be followed in the half-dozen surveys or monographs on particular aspects or problems of medieval Russian literature which he has published during the past twenty years. These works share a number of common features. First, they show that their author has reflected deeply not just on medieval Russian literature but on the literary process itself, on general problems of style, and on the nature of man's response to the written word. At times, indeed, one gains the impression that Russian literature is treated as a kind of laboratory in which the author's general theory of literature can be refined and tested. Conversely, his theoretical conclusions, when applied to specific works of medieval Russian literature, are often highly illuminating. Secondly, these works point to a gradual widening of his geographical horizon: in the late 1950s, for instance, there were already signs that his earlier tendency to view medieval Russian culture in a national context was being superseded by an awareness that Russian literature before the seventeenth century was part of a wider literary tradition which embraced the whole of Eastern and South-Eastern Europe. Thirdly, they illustrate his growing interest in inter-disciplinary research, instanced by his efforts to find common stylistic criteria which would enable us to study literature, folklore, the visual arts and religious thought as related parts of a single cultural whole. Finally, they demonstrate how successful he has been in applying to medieval Russian literature methods which have proved effective in modern literary criticism. This, too, has enhanced the reader's ability to appreciate and enjoy the products of this literature.

The first of these writings, *Vozniknovenie russkoi literatury* (M.–L., 1952), is something of a transitional work. It is not free from chauvinism, and displays some of the nationalistic overtones of Likhachev's early book, *Natsional'noe samosoznanie drevnei Rusi* (M.–L., 1945); yet in several respects it points the way forward to themes of his later work. He rightly emphasizes the importance of 'translated literature', i.e. Old Church Slavonic versions of (in the main) Greek writings, in educating the mind and moulding the outlook of educated Russians in the Kievan period. Too often, in textbooks, this derivative literature is relegated to an introductory chapter and then largely forgotten. Yet these translations, carried out in Bulgaria and to a lesser degree in Russia (they included the Christian Scriptures, liturgical books, patristic and hagiographical works, chronicles and other historical or pseudo-historical writings), nurtured the taste and greatly widened the intellectual horizon of the literate élite; and they stimulated, by a kind of cultural osmosis, the growth of native 'original' literature. Though Likhachev somewhat exaggerates the degree of originality displayed by the Russian translators, he rightly points out that the native ecclesiastical and secular establishment played an active part in this process of transmission, in making a selection in the available corpus of translated works and applying its chosen products to the practical needs of Russian society. This selective borrowing of late antique and medieval Greek literature is seen as an instance of the wider process of Byzantine cultural expansion. To this process he devotes a brief but thought-provoking chapter. Particularly pertinent are his remarks on the social determinants of acculturation, the 'creative' aspects of cultural borrowing, and the relationship between the speed with which Byzantine civilization was absorbed in Russia and the growth within the country of centralized political institutions. His claim, however, that cultural relations between Byzantium and Russia were largely confined to the ruling classes of each country and that the Russian ruling class borrowed Byzantine political ideas, literature, and art in order to increase the authority of the state (pp. 122–7), cannot be accepted without considerable qualifications.

Likhachev's next work of synthesis, *Chelovek v literature drevnei Rusi*, was published in 1958 (a revised edition appeared in 1970). It opens with a challenging question: why do the personalities of Muscovite rulers before the sixteenth century seem so pallid and drearily similar? Was Karamzin justified in complaining that the historian wishing to study the characters of Ivan the Terrible's predecessors is faced with a sandy African desert? Was Klyuchevsky right in asserting that the princes of Moscow before Ivan III are virtually indistinguishable from each other? Not at all, retorts Likhachev. The impression of uniformity is conveyed by the sources; and these reflect the stylistic conventions which in the Middle Ages governed the different literary genres. Interest in human psychology is by no means absent from medieval Russian writings; but it is largely confined to religious and didactic works: the aspirations, feelings and passions (or lack thereof) of saints were necessary to the genre; such psychological inquisitiveness was evidently not regarded as proper in secular princely and royal biographies. It was not, he shows, until the seventeenth century that the art of character portrayal asserted itself in Russian literature, and that writers felt free to demonstrate that good and evil may simultaneously coexist in the same person.

The conventions governing the portrayal of human character varied from period to period, with the result that 'man' in medieval Russian literature appears under different guises. With his characteristic ability to describe a style or movement in a formulaic manner, Likhachev distinguishes the 'monumental historicism' of the period from the eleventh to the thirteenth century, the 'epic style' of the same epoch, the 'expressive-emotional style' of the late fourteenth and fifteenth centuries, and the 'psychological appeasement' of the fifteenth. The argument is made more convincing and vivid by skilfully chosen examples from literature and the visual arts: a noteworthy feature of this book is its conception—to be developed much further in his later works—of a single style common to both fields. Sometimes, as in the twelfth century, the verbal and the visual arts, as far as character portrayal went, were at the same stage of development; in the late Middle Ages literature lagged behind.

In September 1958 Likhachev read a paper to the Fourth International Congress of Slavists in Moscow. Entitled 'Nekotorye zadachi izucheniya vtorogo yuzhnoslavyanskogo vliyaniya v Rossii', it was published two years

later, together with the other Soviet papers presented to the Congress.[11] It is
a pioneering work of great originality and importance. Its ostensible theme
is the 'Second South Slavonic influence', a movement considered to have
affected various aspects of Russian culture in the late fourteenth and the
early fifteenth century, and so called to distinguish it from the earlier,
Bulgarian, wave of influence exerted upon Russia in the tenth and eleventh
centuries. The traditional view, voiced at the turn of the last century by A. I.
Sobolevsky, is that between about 1350 and 1450 a powerful influence was
exerted by the Bulgarians and the Serbs upon the Russians in script, orthography, language and literary style. More particularly, the celebrated
pletenie sloves ('braiding of words') employed with such virtuosity at the turn
of the fourteenth century by the Russian hagiographer Epiphanius, a style
distinguished by its mannered ornateness, rhetorical diction and overt
euphonic effects, is held to have been inspired by the linguistic reform and
literary programme of Euthymius, Patriarch of Bulgaria from 1375 to 1393.
Much, however, in the history of this movement remains mysterious and
controversial. How far did Epiphanius build on earlier Russian literary
traditions? What were the origin and the precise nature of Euthymius's
reform? How much did both men owe to the influence of Byzantium?

Likhachev's thesis may be summarized as follows.[12] This 'influence', when
examined more closely, is seen as a manifestation of a cosmopolitan movement which, in the second half of the fourteenth century, powerfully affected
the literature of the whole of Eastern and South-Eastern Europe. Its characteristic products were ornate rhetorical panegyrics and Lives of saints. The
theoretical basis of this movement was laid in Bulgaria by the Patriarch
Euthymius who not only employed the new panegyrical style in his own
writings, but also, it would seem, laid down the rules to be followed in
translating Byzantine texts into Church Slavonic: they included a return to
the grammar, orthography and punctuation of the original translations of
Cyril and Methodius, and the need to remodel the morphology and syntax
of Church Slavonic as closely as possible on Greek. This antiquarian, utopian
and philhellenic movement was itself but one aspect of a cultural resurgence
in the fields of literature, art and religion which in the fourteenth century
spread from the Byzantine Empire to the Balkans and Russia. It was closely
connected with the Palaeologan school of Byzantine painting on the one
hand, and with the mystical theology of Byzantine Hesychasm on the other.
In Russia this movement found expression in the writings of Epiphanius (who,
building on native traditions, perfected the technique of 'word-braiding'),
in the frescoes at Volotovo and in those of Theophanes the Greek, and in the
spiritual traditions of St. Sergius's Monastery of the Holy Trinity. In its
élitism, antiquarianism, high regard for scholarship, philhellenism, and
interest in human psychology and the natural world, this movement
resembles the European Renaissance. Yet it was too religious and too

---

[11] *Issledovaniya po slavyanskomu literaturovedeniyu i fol'kloristike* (M., 1960).
[12] It was further developed in his article 'Predvozrozhdenie na Rusi v kontse XIV—pervoi
polovine XV veka', in *Literaturu epokhi Vozrozhdeniya i problemy vsemirnoi literatury* (M., 1967),
136–82.

'medieval' in character to deserve that name. It may more appropriately be described as a 'pre-Renaissance'.

No detailed critique of Likhachev's wide-ranging thesis can be attempted here. He makes no claim to have solved any of the complex problems he has raised.[13] Two of them may be briefly examined for their general interest. The first is purely literary. While it is probable that late medieval Russian literature was 'influenced' by the Euthymian school of Trnovo, and the latter by the style of fourteenth-century Byzantine hagiography, this double connexion has not yet been firmly established. Only by a thorough linguistic comparison of the writings of the Byzantine Patriarchs Kallistos and Philo-theos with those of Euthymius and his Slavonic disciples and of the Russian writers of the late fourteenth and the fifteenth centuries can the theory of a direct transmission of the 'new style' from Byzantium to Russia via the Balkan Slavs be accurately tested. This comparative analysis has not yet been made. However, the likelihood that the true picture was more complex is enhanced by the fact—of which Likhachev is fully aware—that Epiphanius's style owed something at least to the rhetorical traditions of Kievan Russia, and that evidence of the literary manner associated with Euthymius's late fourteenth-century Bulgarian school has been detected in thirteenth-century Serbia.

The second problem arises from Likhachev's belief in the connexions between the East European literary movement, Palaeologan painting, and Hesychast theology. In his search for links between literature and the visual arts he resorts to the method of analogy: 'abstract psychologism', which he regards as a basic trait of the South Slavonic and Russian panegyrical style, is also, in his view, characteristic of fourteenth-century Palaeologan paint-ing;[14] on the other hand, terms which art historians have used to describe this artistic style—emotional expressiveness, an enhanced sense of rhythm, a liking for movement and dramatic tension—can also be applied to the writings of the Balkan and Russian 'panegyrical' school, above all to those of Epiphanius. But Likhachev is too cautious a scholar to draw hasty con-clusions from these apparent similarities. 'This connexion' [between Russian fourteenth-century painting and literature], he writes, 'may of course be noted only in the most general form: [at those points] where literature and painting come into contact in a [common] artistic vision of the world and in the sphere of ideology.'[15] It is a significant *caveat*. He seems to be implying that further, and more specific, criteria must be discovered before we can successfully attempt a common stylistic evaluation of the verbal and the visual arts. Can such a criterion be discovered to bridge the gap?

It is in 'the sphere of ideology' that Likhachev seeks for such a bridge. For his present purpose the ideology on which he has pinned his hopes is Hesy-chasm. The term is used today in a variety of meanings.[16] Here it will be

---

[13] 'Nekotorye zadachi', 96.

[14] Ibid. 129; 'Predvozrozhdenie', 170.

[15] 'Nekotorye zadachi', 131; 'Predvozrozhdenie', 172.

[16] See J. Meyendorff, 'O vizantiiskom isikhazme i ego roli v kul'turnom i istoricheskom razvitii Vostochnoi Evropy v XIV v.', *Trudy Otdela drevnerusskoi literatury*, xxix (1974), 291–305. The modern literature on hesychasm is immense: see D. Stiernon, 'Bulletin sur le Palamisme', *Revue des études byzantines*, xxx (1972), 231–341.

sufficient to note that Hesychasm (the term is derived from the Greek *hesychia*, 'quiet') denotes in the East Christian spiritual life the state of recollection and inner silence which follows man's victory over his passions and leads him, through the practice of contemplative prayer, to the vision of God. This 'prayer of the mind' or 'prayer of the heart' became linked in the late Middle Ages with the frequent repetition of the 'Jesus prayer' ('Lord Jesus Christ, Son of God, have mercy upon me') and with certain bodily exercises (such as the regulation of breathing) designed to aid spiritual concentration. The practice of Hesychasm, whose roots go back to the earliest traditions of Christian asceticism, gained wide currency in the fourteenth century through the influence of hermitages and monasteries of Mount Athos and the teaching and example of a great spiritual master, St. Gregory of Sinai. Gregory established between 1330 and 1346, on the boundary between the Greek and the Slav worlds, a Balkan monastic community, whose influence spread far and wide through Eastern Europe.[17] Hesychasm received a weighty theological justification in the teaching of St. Gregory Palamas (1296–1359) concerning the Uncreated Light which illumines him who is spiritually transformed through the practice of the 'prayer of the heart'. This light, Gregory taught, is one of the 'energies' or 'operations' of God, distinct from His essence, yet capable of uniting man to the divine nature.[18] In the fourteenth and fifteenth centuries Hesychasm, whose doctrines were declared to be Orthodox by the Byzantine Church, became a cosmopolitan movement, which affected Byzantium, Bulgaria, Serbia, Rumania, and Russia and greatly helped to cement closer links between the different parts of the 'Byzantine Commonwealth'.[19]

That a connexion existed between Hesychasm and the East European literary movement of the late Middle Ages cannot be doubted. Euthymius and his leading Slavonic disciples, who carried their master's teachings to the monasteries and royal courts of Eastern Europe, were strongly committed Hesychasts. Among the many translations from Greek into Church Slavonic carried out by scholars of the 'Euthymian' school, pride of place was accorded to spiritual writers popular in Hesychast circles, such as John of the Ladder, Symeon the New Theologian, Gregory of Sinai and Gregory Palamas. The ideal of *hesychia* was extolled in 'Euthymian' hagiographical works. Likhachev has no difficulty in showing that in ideological terms 'the Second South Slavonic influence' cannot be understood without reference to Hesychasm.[20]

The connexion between Hesychasm and Palaeologan art raises a more difficult problem. On general grounds it seems highly unlikely that this art, which was primarily religious in content and which spread throughout

[17] See K. Ware, 'The Jesus Prayer in St. Gregory of Sinai', *Eastern Churches Review*, iv (1972), 3–22.

[18] See J. Meyendorff, *Introduction à l'étude de Grégoire Palamas* (Paris, 1959).

[19] See G. M. Prokhorov, 'Isikhazm i obshchestvennaya mysl' v Vostochnoi Evrope v XIV v.', *TODRL*, xxiii (1968); A.-E. Tachiaos, 'Le mouvement hésychaste pendant les dernières décennies du XIVᵉ siècle', *Kleronomia*, vi, 1 (Thessaloniki, 1974), 113–30.

[20] In this writer's opinion, Likhachev has not succeeded in convincingly demonstrating the influence of Hesychasm on the style (as distinct from the content) of the late medieval literary movement. See 'Nekotorye zadachi', 134–5, and 'Predvozrozhdenie', 163–4.

Eastern and South-Eastern Europe, escaped the influence of the equally cosmopolitan and influential Hesychast movement. But is there concrete evidence in the iconography or the style of Palaeologan painting of the influence of Hesychast ideas? The question has been frequently debated of late, and much ingenuity and learning have been expended in efforts to detect signs of Hesychast theology in Byzantine monumental painting of the fourteenth and fifteenth centuries.[21] In this writer's opinion these attempts have not so far been successful. Likhachev's cursory references to the work of Theophanes and of the Volotovo master are not convincing.[22] The problem is not necessarily insoluble. Byzantine religious art, at least since the iconoclastic controversies of the eighth and ninth centuries, had a strong doctrinal and intellectual component.[23] But here again, as with the relationship between painting and literary style, specific connexions are hard to trace. No doubt further search for satisfactory common theological and aesthetic criteria is needed. Perhaps this search will be facilitated if we think of Hesychasm less as a self-contained system of thought which developed in fourteenth-century Byzantium and more in terms of its true nature: an organic development of the age-long tradition of Eastern Christian spirituality.

Likhachev's failure to demonstrate the influence of Hesychasm on the style of the late medieval literature of Russia and the Balkan Slavonic countries and on Palaeologan art in no way diminishes his merit in carrying out the most comprehensive study yet undertaken of the 'Second South Slavonic influence', and in placing this movement—for the first time—in a convincing context. All future students of this movement will now have to take as their starting-point his lucid definition: 'we are confronted with the phenomenon of a single intellectual movement, sufficiently powerful to embrace various countries and sufficiently profound to have affected simultaneously literature, writing, painting, and religion'.[24]

This cosmopolitan, late medieval movement, which affected the Byzantine Empire, Bulgaria, Serbia, Russia, the Caucasian lands, and to some extent Asia Minor,[25] Likhachev proposes to call 'the East European pre-Renaissance'. The appropriateness of this terminology has been called in question.[26]

---

[21] See the bibliography in D. Obolensky, *The Byzantine Commonwealth: Eastern Europe, 500–1453* (1971), 413 to which must now be added: M. V. Alpatov, 'Iskusstvo Feofana Greka i uchenie isikhastov, *Vizantiiskii vremennik*, xxxiii (1972), 190–202; J. Meyendorff, 'O vizantiiskom isikhazme' (n. 16), 297–301; J. Meyendorff, 'Spiritual Trends in Byzantium in the late thirteenth and early fourteenth centuries', in *The Kariye Djami*, ed. P. A. Underwood, iv (1975), 105–6.

[22] 'Nekotorye zadachi', 132–3; 'Predvozrozhdenie', 173–4.

[23] Meyendorff, op. cit. (n. 16), 300.

[24] Ibid. 138.

[25] Ibid. 138. Surprisingly Likhachev omits the Rumanian principalities, whose educated classes played an important role in this movement. See E. Turdeanu, *La littérature bulgare du XIVe siècle et sa diffusion dans les pays roumains* (Paris, 1947). In a later work, however, Likhachev made amends for this omission: see below, n. 30.

[26] Notably by R. Picchio, who proposes to substitute the term 'Slavonic Orthodox revival': '"Prerinascimento esteuropeo" e "Rinascita slava ortodossa"', *Ricerche Slavistiche*, vi (1958), 185–99. He also unaccountably omits the Rumanians. Cf. Likhachev's reply to Picchio, 'Neskol'ko zamechanii po povodu stat'i Rikkardo Pikkio', *TODRL*, xvii (1961), 675–8, and Picchio's rejoinder, 'Die historisch-philologische Bedeutung der kirchenslavischen Tradition', *Die Welt der Slaven*, vii (1962), 20–3.

Some scholars, on the other hand, have shown willingness to accept it.[27] Like any formula seeking to encapsulate a complex phenomenon, it invites reservations. But, as an empirical category, it ought surely to be allowed to stand the test of time. And it has at least the merit of suggesting legitimate parallels between the late medieval culture of Eastern and Western Europe and of drawing attention to the fact that, for different reasons, neither Russia nor the Graeco–Slavonic world of the Balkans was ever to experience a full 'Renaissance'.

Likhachev's interest in the relationship between the verbal and visual arts reappears in his next book, *Poetika drevnerusskoi literatury* (L., 1967, revised edition, 1971). His chapter on this subject[28] is full of illuminating remarks. Some of them show that his search for analogies between writing and painting has become more concrete. A good example of co-operation between the two is provided by inscriptions on icons. These, he shows, are closely bound up with the icon's aesthetic, narrative, and doctrinal design. They are part of its ornamental pattern; their wording, when they are quotations from the Life of the saint represented on the icon, sometimes complements the story told in colours; and, by often appearing with their verbs changed from the past to the present tense, they serve to emphasize the timelessness of the icon, which depicts not just a past event, but an eternal present.

In other respects, too, *Poetika drevnerusskoi literatury* develops themes of Likhachev's earlier works. This is true of his concept of 'literary etiquette' which compelled the medieval writer to adhere to ritualized stylistic conventions governing the particular situation he wrote about;[29] and of the section on *nestilizatsionnye podrazhaniya*, with its further discussion of the relationship between the *Zadonshchina* and the *Slovo o polku Igoreve*. And it will remain one of his most impressive achievements to have demonstrated, more persuasively than any other scholar, that Russian literature until the seventeenth century was not a self-contained unit, but part of a supra-national literary tradition, based on the Church Slavonic language, which was the common heritage of the Eastern Slavs, the Bulgarians, the Serbs and the Rumanians.[30]

The later, 'theoretical', works of Likhachev may be likened to successive stages on a voyage of discovery, whose aim is to help us appreciate and enjoy medieval Russian literature in the light of his reflections on the problems of creative writing. In each of these works he seems in turn to pause in order to review his previous work, take stock of his earlier conclusions, draw breath and then set out to explore new horizons. This is especially true of his *Razvitie russkoi literatury X–XVII vekov* (1973), a book which contains the quintessence of his thinking to date. His declared aim is to provide 'a few generalizations for the construction of a future theoretical history of Russian literature from

[27] See the perceptive study by R. R. Milner-Gulland, 'Russia's Lost Renaissance', in *Literature and Western Civilization*, iii, ed. D. Daiches and A. K. Thorlby (1973), 435–68.

[28] 1971 ed., 24–41.

[29] 'The medieval reader, as he reads, participates in a sense in a ceremony, includes himself in this ceremony, is present at an "action", a kind of "liturgy" . . . The writer is the master of ceremonies.' Ibid. 111.

[30] Ibid. 6.

the tenth to the seventeenth century'. What we have here in fact is a refined and sophisticated approach to the problem of literary styles and periods. Some of the ground is by now familiar: the relationship between verbal and visual art, the influence of Hesychasm on literature, the nature of the East European cultural movement of the late Middle Ages are discussed yet again.

One of the novel and most thought-provoking sections of *Razvitie russkoi literatury* embodies the results of the author's recent thinking on the nature of Byzantine influence on medieval Russian literature. He introduces two concepts which in this context prove useful and illuminating: 'literary transplantation' and 'intermediary literature'. The over-used term 'influence', when applied to the impact of Byzantium on medieval Russia, is, he points out, inadequate. Did Byzantine Christianity 'influence' Russian paganism? Did Byzantine literature 'influence' Russian literature at the time when the latter was being born? Surely in both these cases a more comprehensive process was at work. Often, Likhachev observes, works translated from Greek into Slavonic underwent a gradual change in their adopted countries, acquiring fresh features and developing local variants. This justifies the analogy between literary 'translation' and the botanical process of 'transplantation': Byzantine writings transplanted to Eastern Europe brought forth creative offshoots which continued to live and grow in their new soil. Transplantation was thus accompanied by changes in the borrowed product, and this process was possible only because the society and the culture of the 'receiving' country—in this case Russia—were at that time in a state of rapid change.

Likhachev's concept of 'intermediary literature' is used to explain the role of Old Church Slavonic (after *c.* 1100, Church Slavonic) in providing a channel for the regular flow of culture from the Greek-speaking world to the Slav countries of Eastern Europe, as well as a bond linking the different recensions of Slavonic literature to themselves and to Byzantium. This role was greatly facilitated by the close relationship which Old Church Slavonic had to medieval Greek on the one hand, and to the spoken languages of the Slav peoples on the other. 'Intermediary literature' is defined by Likhachev as 'a literature which not only "lets through" (*propuskayushchaya cherez sebya*) individual works of other literatures, but builds up a special international fund of writings which exist simultaneously on the national territories of a number of countries as a single, developing whole' (p. 24). This fund of translated literature became the common heritage of the Orthodox Slavonic and Rumanian peoples. Whether in the lifetime of Cyril and Methodius and their disciples, or in the period of 'the Second South Slavonic influence', it was, in Likhachev's terminology, 'the Slavonic recension of Byzantine culture'.[31]

Byzantium's contribution to the cultural life of the East European peoples is a subject that has recently been attracting the growing interest of historians. In all further studies of this subject Likhachev's work is bound to carry much weight.

[31] Some of Likhachev's views on the Byzantine impact upon Russian culture were developed in a preliminary form in his article 'The Type and Character of the Byzantine Influence on Old Russian Literature', *Oxford Slavonic Papers*, xiii (1967), 16–32.

This survey of the principal works[32] of Dmitry Sergeevich Likhachev has been confined to his medieval studies. In some of his later writings, notably in *Razvitie russkoi literatury*, he pursues his themes as far as the eighteenth century. In some respects his general approach to literary problems is not unlike that of Dmitry Chizhevsky.[33] But in his treatment of textological problems, his perception of the relations between literature and painting, and his inquiries into problems of style he has an originality and a profundity that are all his own.

[32] His recent book, *Velikoe nasledie: klassicheskie proizvedeniya literatury drevnei Rusi* (M., 1975), is a most useful survey, which comes nearest to being a conventional history of medieval Russian literature. It is thus somewhat different in character from the 'general' books reviewed in this section.

[33] See, however, his critical remarks on Chizhevsky's views in *Razvitie russkoi literatury*, 188 ff.

Law and Social Change in Medieval Russia: The *Zakon sudnyi lyudem* as a Case Study

By A. M. KLEIMOLA

EVENTS of recent years have focused renewed interest on the relationship between law and social change. The traditional view sees law as simply the codification of what the American nineteenth-century sociologist William Graham Sumner called pre-existing 'folkways' and 'mores'. The newer view sees law as not simply a reflection of the past, but as a dynamic force in shaping the future. The problem has special relevance for the historian of medieval Russia, since much of the surviving source material consists of legal codes and documents. This study of the role and significance of the *Zakon sudnyi lyudem*, or *Judicial Law for Laymen*, is intended as a case study of the larger problem of applying legal analysis to illuminate historical developments.

The ninth-century protograph of the *Judicial Law* is generally regarded as 'one of the oldest monuments of Slavonic juridical thought'.[1] The earliest extant version is the so-called 'short' redaction found in the Novgorod *Kormchaya* of the late thirteenth century. The 'short' redaction has been the subject of extensive scholarly investigation. But most of this work has focused upon the question of the national origins of the ninth-century protograph.

The earliest students of the problem concluded that the original code had been compiled in Bulgaria shortly after the conversion of Prince Boris to Christianity in 865.[2] The chief modern defenders of this thesis are Bulgarians, and they base their argument mainly upon so-called 'historical necessity'. According to this view, the document was compiled in Bulgaria in 866–8 to serve the needs of a newly Christianized society that was fighting to eliminate the vestiges of paganism and bring old practices into conformity with Christian principles. Boris's law-makers consulted both the *Ecloga*, the eighth-century Byzantine law code issued by the Isaurian emperors, and the 'answers of Pope Nicholas', responses from the Pope to a series of questions on 'civil law' addressed to him by Boris before the Bulgarian ruler finally

---

[1] M. N. Tikhomirov, *ed.*, *Zakon sudnyi lyudem kratkoi redaktsii* (M., 1961), 3 (this edition hereafter cited as *ZSL kratkoi*); V. Ganev, *Zakon" soudnyi lyud'm"* (Sofia, 1959), 63.

[2] For example, G. A. Rozenkampf, *Obozrenie Kormchei knigi v istoricheskom vide* (M., 1829); V. Vasil'evsky, 'Zakonodatel'stvo ikonobortsev', *Zhurnal Ministerstva narodnogo prosveshcheniya*, cxcix (1878), 258–309; N. S. Suvorov, *Sledy zapadno-katolicheskogo tserkovnogo prava v pamyatnikakh drevnego russkogo prava* (Yaroslavl', 1888), published in *Vremennik Demidovskogo yuridicheskogo litseya*, xlviii–xlix; T. Florinsky, 'Drevneishii pamyatnik bolgarskogo prava', *Sbornik statei po istorii prava* (Kiev, 1904), 404–29.

opted for Byzantine rather than Roman Christianity. Proponents of the Bulgarian theory claim that this 'Bulgarian document' served as a model for later law codes in other countries, notably the Kievan *Russkaya Pravda*.[3]

On the other hand, Czech scholars have argued that the *Judicial Law* was originally compiled in Moravia. They base their argument primarily upon linguistic evidence within the text. They claim that the 'short' redaction is filled with typical Moravian—and not Bulgarian—words and phrases, that the misunderstanding and miscopying of these Moravian terms by the later Russian scribes account for some of the obscure passages in the text of the 'short' redaction that have confounded students, and that the Russian version contains numerous similarities and parallels with other ninth-century Moravian works such as the *vita* of Methodius, the Kiev Missal, the Freising texts, Methodius's translation of the Nomocanon and the homily in *Clozianus* ascribed to him. As for the author of the *Judicial Law*, proponents of the Moravian theory have wavered between Cyril and Methodius, with more recent studies favouring Methodius.[4]

The third major theory on the origins of the *Judicial Law*—the so-called 'Macedonian theory'—has been put forth by S. V. Troitsky of Belgrade. Troitsky agrees that the compiler of the *Judicial Law* was Methodius, but disagrees with the suggestion that Moravia was the code's place of origin. In Troitsky's view, Methodius drafted the *Judicial Law* for Byzantium's Slav militiamen in Strymon (Macedonia), probably in the decade 830–40, when Methodius was serving as military governor there. Troitsky argues that the haphazard and incomplete contents of the *Judicial Law* do make sense when read as a 'warrior code' whose provisions apply only to males, particularly to males of fighting age. And Troitsky contends that the very term *lyudi*, which figures in the code's title as well as text, should be understood as 'warriors'.[5]

At least three other, less convincing theories on the origin of the *Judicial Law*—the Russian, Serbian, and Pannonian—have appeared at different times and places.[6] But given the state of the existing documentation, no

---

[3] M. Andreev, (1) 'Yavlyaetsya li "Zakon soudnyi lyud'm'"' drevnebolgarskim yuridicheskim pamyatnikom?', *Slavyanskii arkhiv*, 1959, pp. 17–18; idem, (2), 'Sur l'origine du "Zakon sudnyi ljudem" (Loi pour juger les gens)', *Revue des études sud-est européennes*, i (1963), 335–7; Ganev, op. cit. (n. 1), 613–15; L. V. Milov, 'Novoe issledovanie o Zakone sudnom lyudem', *Slavyanskii arkhiv*, 1961, p. 53; for a comprehensive bibliography on the Bulgarian theory, see V. Procházka, 'Le Zakon" sudnyj' ljud'm" et la Grande Moravie', *Byzantinoslavica*, xxviii (1967), 360, nn. 4–5.

[4] J. Vašica, (1) 'Origine cyrillo-méthodienne du plus ancien code slave dit "Zakon sudnyj ljudem" ', *Byzantinoslavica*, xii (1951), 154–74; idem, (2) 'Kirillo-Mefodievskie yuridicheskie pamyatniki', *Voprosy slavyanskogo yazykoznaniya*, vii (1963), 12–33; idem, (3) 'Velkomoravský původ Zakona sudného ljudem' in: *Literární památky epochy velkomoravské*, 73–84 (the same work contains a Czech translation of the text of the *Judicial Law* [pp. 149–56] and a commentary on the text [pp. 156–69]); V. Procházka, op. cit. (n. 3), *Byzantinoslavica*, xxviii (1967), 359–75, and xxix (1968), 112–50.

[5] S. V. Troitsky, (1) 'Sv. Mefody kak slavyanskii zakonodatel'', *Bogoslovskie trudy*, ii (1961), 96, 100–11; idem, (2) 'Svyatoi Mefody kak slavyanskii zakonodatel'', *Zhurnal Moskovskoi patriarkhii*, 1961 no. 1, pp. 51, 54–6; idem, (3) 'Svyatoi Mefody ili bolgarskii knyaz' Boris sostavil Zakon sudnyi lyudem?', *Bogoslovskie trudy*, iv (1968), 120–1.

[6] I. D. Belyaev, *Lektsii po istorii russkogo zakonodatel'stva* (M., 1879), 209–10; Procházka, op. cit. (nn. 3–4), 124; Andreev, op. cit. (1) (n. 3), 10.

definitive resolution of the question of national origin is possible.[7] Unfortunately, the debate over this problem has distracted attention from other more important questions. Whatever the origin of the *Judicial Law* in one or more of the newly Christianized Slav states, it was not in any of these areas that the code would play a role of lasting importance. Methodius's followers were banished from Moravia soon after his death, and the *Judicial Law* leaves no traces in later Czech law.[8] Nor has anyone demonstrated a subsequent role for the *Judicial Law* in Bulgaria or Macedonia. Only in Russia did the code live on.

The 'short' redaction has survived in scores of Russian manuscripts; over fifty of the earliest copies were studied by the late M. N. Tikhomirov and his collaborators in preparing their printed edition of selected manuscript texts.[9] In Russia the 'short' redaction was incorporated in the *Kormchaya kniga*, the nomocanon of the Russian church. And, in that same country, a second version—the 'expanded' redaction—of the *Judicial Law* appeared. It was in Russia, then, that the first Slavonic law code was to play a major role and exert a lasting influence.

Yet examination of the provisions of the extant Russian texts raises questions about what role—and what influence—the *Judicial Law* had. The 'short' redaction consists of 31, 32, or 33 'chapters', depending on the numbering system used in a given manuscript.[10] Most of these chapters were derived from the eighth-century Byzantine *Ecloga*.[11] But the borrowing was highly selective. The compiler of the 'short' redaction took most of his materials from a single chapter of the *Ecloga*, chapter 17. And few of the provisions of the 'short' redaction were direct translations from the *Ecloga*; the majority contain significant modifications. Scholars in the Slavonic countries have tended to explain these modifications as representing an enlightened and humane attempt to soften and make more equitable the Byzantine code's harsh provisions. Thus, for example, the chapters specifying fasts and penances for wrong-doers have been interpreted as an attempt to rehabilitate rather than simply punish the wrong-doer. And whereas the *Ecloga* assigned

[7] At the present time proponents of each theory seem largely concerned with discrediting the opposition, often by stating that rival hypotheses 'lack foundation' or reflect nationalist bias; see, for example, Vašica, op. cit. (2) (n. 4), 32; Andreev, op. cit. (2) (n. 3), 337–8; P. I. Žužek, *Kormčaja Kniga: Studies on the Chief Code of Russian Canon Law* (Orientalia Christiana Analecta, 168) (Rome, 1964), 19–20; Troitsky, op. cit. (3) (n. 5), 122, 124; and idem, 'Apostol slavyanstva sv. Mefody kak kanonist', *Zhurnal Moskovskoi patriarkhii*, 1958, pp. 41, 44–5.

[8] Procházka, op. cit. (nn. 3–4), 150.

[9] *ZSL kratkoi*, 7.

[10] References in this paper are to the chapters of the 'short' redaction as numbered in the earliest surviving Russian copy of the text; for the text from the Novgorod *Kormchaya*, see *ZSL kratkoi*, 35–45, 115–27.

[11] On the sources of the various chapters, see Žužek, *Kormčaja Kniga* (n. 7), 86–7, and T. Saturník, *Příspěvky k šíření byzantského práva u Slovanů* (Rozpravy České akademie věd a umění, Třída i, no. 64) (Prague, 1922), 143–54. For the text of the *Ecloga*, see K. E. Zachariä a Lingenthal, *Collectio librorum juris graeco-romani ineditorum* (Lipsiae, 1852), the English translation by E. H. Freshfield, *A Manual of Roman Law: The Ecloga* (Cambridge, 1926), and the Russian translation, by E. E. Lipshits, *Ekloga: vizantiiskii zakonodatel'nyi svod VIII veka* (M., 1965).

all fines to the state coffers, the *Judicial Law* (ch. 1 and 4) provides that such fines be given to the poor.[12] Only in respect of crimes against the church does the 'short' redaction of the *Judicial Law* specify more severe penalties than the *Ecloga*: chapter 18 provides that anyone who enters a church to apprehend a person who has taken refuge there shall receive a punishment 'almost twelve times' as severe as that specified in the *Ecloga*,[13] and chapter 30 prescribes slavery or flogging for any offender who steals from a church.

Another, and more difficult, problem in dealing with the 'short' redaction is its extremely heterogeneous character. The first chapter proclaims the supremacy of God's justice and prescribes penalties for pagans. But then the code goes on to deal with: the testimony of witnesses (ch. 2, 20, 22); distribution of war booty (ch. 3); sexual morality, marital relations, and divorce (ch. 4–15, 33); arson (ch. 16–17); asylum (ch. 18); self-help (ch. 19); a captive's right to regain freedom by repaying his ransom or by working off his debt to his purchaser (ch. 21); what should be done with repatriated prisoners-of-war who have renounced Christianity in captivity (ch. 23); offences involving horses and livestock (ch. 24–5, 28); types of theft and a master's responsibility for theft by his slave (ch. 26–7, 29, 30); illegal enslavement (ch. 31); and concealment of another's slave (ch. 32).

Thus, there are elements of canon law, military law, civil law, and criminal law, together with guidelines for civil and criminal procedure, all combined in one short code. Several chapters (4, 6–10, 12, 15) provide as punishment for offences against morality fines or corporal punishment *and* penance. Chapter 7, for example, decrees that anyone who fornicates with a nun shall have his nose cut off in accordance with civil law, as well as be given a fast of fifteen years in accordance with ecclesiastical law. Some chapters deal with matters—such as the division of war booty—that appear to be purely secular; others deal with questions that fell within church jurisdiction (e.g. sexual mores, marital relations, and provisions for fasting and penance); still others set forth regulations which could be applicable in both civil and ecclesiastical courts (e.g. injunctions against perjury, prohibitions against hearsay evidence, or requirements for witnesses).

The problem is further complicated by the unevenness and 'fragmentary' nature of the provisions. In relation to certain offences the code goes into considerable detail; about others it has literally nothing to say. For example, although the code touches on a variety of civil and criminal offences, there are many notable gaps, the most obvious being the lack of any provision relating to murder. Consequently, the contents of the 'short' redaction provide little clue as to the purpose behind its compilation or the use for which it was intended.

The code's opening paragraph, in contrast to such other legal documents as the Byzantine *Ecloga* or the Kievan *Russkaya Pravda*, contains no reference to its having been issued in the reign of a particular ruler and provides no

---

[12] For such views, see, *inter alia*, Troitsky, op. cit. (2) (n. 5), 56–7, and op. cit. (1) (n. 5), 90; Andreev, op. cit. (1) (n. 3), 14; Procházka, op. cit. (nn. 3–4), 326–7; Lipshits, *Ekloga* (n. 11), 164, 176–86.

[13] Troitsky, op. cit. (1) (n. 5), 106–7.

information concerning the time and circumstances of its compilation and promulgation. Instead, the 'short' redaction's title and first chapter give credit to a mysterious emperor, 'Saint Constantine'. Since 'Constantine' has been variously identified as Constantine the Great, or Constantine V, son of the Byzantine emperor Leo the Isaurian, or St. Constantine-Cyril, the brother of Methodius, erroneously promoted to the rank of emperor by later copyists,[14] the introduction of the text provides no clue as to its origin.

Nor is there any direct information on the *Judicial Law* during the four centuries that elapsed between its original compilation in the ninth century and the appearance of the earliest extant text in Russia in the Novgorod *Kormchaya* of the late thirteenth century. But textual and linguistic evidence does shed some light upon the history of the code in Russia. Textual evidence indicates that the *Judicial Law* was not part of the original manuscript that served as the basis for the Novgorod *Kormchaya*, but that the 'short' redaction was inserted along with such other supplemental materials as the *Russkaya Pravda* in an attempt to bring together in a single codex all the available legal texts.[15] And it appears that by the late thirteenth century the *Judicial Law* was already an archaic work. The differences between variant texts of the 'short' redaction indicate that the phraseology was in certain places unintelligible to the scribes who copied it. The word *kupetra* ('godmother' or 'godparent'), for example, apparently presented particular difficulties. Whereas chapter 8 in the Novgorod text starts with the statement, 'If anyone takes his godmother (*kupetra*) as his wife', the compiler of the Ustyug *Kormchaya* managed to turn this into 'if anyone buys a female slave to take as his wife' (*izhe kupit' rabu*), while yet another scribe sought to avoid use of *kupetra* by reworking the passage to read 'if anyone takes any of his female relatives' or 'if anyone takes his female relative or his own sister' (*izhe uzhiku etru svoyu* or *izhe uzhiku i [se]stru svoyu*).[16] This evidence suggests that the code probably reached Russia soon after its conversion to Byzantine Christianity in the late tenth century.[17]

At the same time, the linguistic evidence also indicates that the *Judicial Law* was still being used in Russia at the time the surviving texts were copied. These scribal errors—and other changes—were the result of the scribes' efforts to clarify obscure passages through substituting words or phrases which would be understood by contemporary Russian readers. Such attempts at modernization of the text indicate that the compilers who included the *Judicial Law* in their collections regarded it as a work having some significance in Russian juridical practice.[18] And the 'short' redaction

---

[14] F. Dvornik, 'Byzantine Political Ideas in Kievan Russia', *Dumbarton Oaks Papers*, ix–x (1956), 78; Andreev, op. cit. (2) (n. 3), 338; Troitsky, op. cit. (1) (n. 5), 87–8; Vašica, op. cit. (1) (n. 4), 170–1.
[15] On the history of the Novgorod *Kormchaya*, see ZSL kratkoi, 8–14, and Ya. N. Shchapov, 'K istorii teksta Novgorodskoi Sinodal'noi Kormchei', *Istoriko-arkheologicheskii sbornik* (M., 1962), 295–301.
[16] See ZSL kratkoi, 22, 42, 49.
[17] Dvornik, op. cit. (n.14), 77; M. N. Tikhomirov, *ed.*, *Zakon sudnyi lyudem prostrannoi i svodnoi redaktsii* (M., 1961), 27 (hereafter cited as ZSL prostrannoi).
[18] ZSL kratkoi, 18. Some examples of such changes include using the more common *penyaz'* for 'money' in place of *st'lyaz'*, or writing *pobeda na vragi* rather than *pobeda brani*.

of the *Judicial Law* continued to play a prominent role in medieval Russian law. The text was copied, modified, and recopied over the centuries, and finally included in Patriarch Nikon's printed *Kormchaya* of 1653.[19]

While the evidence shows the continuing interest in the *Judicial Law* in Russia during the thirteenth and fourteenth centuries, the question remains —what purpose did the code serve? The answer to this question must be sought in the role of the church within medieval Russian society.

From the time Russia adopted Christianity in the late tenth century, the church was engaged in a long struggle to eliminate the vestiges of paganism and establish Christian principles of morality in Russian society The problem was most acute in the north Russian territories. The new faith spread with relative slowness in the Novgorod lands in the face of the influence of neighbouring pagan peoples and the continued strength of the old cults. Christianity apparently made little advance in these north Russian areas up to the twelfth century, and even after it took root firmly, there is ample evidence of the persistence of pagan practices in the region as late as the fifteenth and sixteenth centuries.[20] Given this problem, the continued interest in the *Judicial Law* can be understood in terms of the applicability of many of the provisions to establishing new rules of morality in a society recently converted to the Christian faith.[21] This conclusion is reinforced by the connexion of a large number of the surviving copies with the north Russian territories.

The church also may have found another practical use for the *Judicial Law*. Codes of this sort—such as the Greek *Nomocanon*, or the *Ecloga*, or the *Procheiron*—were held up as a model for a secular ruler to follow, especially if existing Russian custom or law was not in accord with the teachings of the Christian faith.[22] And there is a resemblance in content and arrangement of material between the 'short' redaction of the *Judicial Law* and the Church Statute attributed to the Kievan ruler Yaroslav the Wise.[23] Because of the difficulties of dating the documents, their precise relationship cannot be

---

[19] On the printed *Kormchaya*, see Žužek, *Kormčaja Kniga* (n. 7), 52–101. Žužek also discusses some ecclesiastical court cases from the eighteenth century in which the Synod cited the *Judicial Law* among other precedents (pp. 246–7, 256–7); for the texts of these cases, see *Polnoe sobranie postanovlenii i rasporyazhenii po Vedomstvu Pravoslavnogo Ispovedaniya* (19 vols., Spb., 1870–1915), vi, 2153, 2209; vii, 2308; and viii, 2788.

[20] Ya. N. Shchapov, *Knyazheskie ustavy i tserkov' v drevnei Rusi XI–XIV vv.* (M., 1972), 46–8; *Akty, sobrannye v bibliotekakh i arkhivakh Rossiiskoi imperii Arkheograficheskoyu ekspeditsieyu*, i (Spb., 1836), no. 369, pp. 461–2; *Dopolneniya k Aktam istoricheskim*, i (Spb., 1846), no. 28, pp. 27–30, and no. 43, pp. 57–60.

[21] This point has been made by scholars dealing with the origins of the code, e.g. Andreev, op. cit. (1) (n. 3), 6–16, and op. cit. (2) (n. 3), 333–5; Vašica, op. cit. (2) (n. 4), 28; Procházka, op. cit. (nn. 3–4), 142–6. But they have failed to see the relevance to the Russian situation.

[22] N. Kalachov, 'O znachenii Kormchei v sisteme drevnego russkogo prava', *Chteniya v Imperatorskom Obshchestve istorii i drevnostei rossiiskikh*, iii, no. 3 (1847), 9–10, 50–1 (n. 21), 61–71 (n. 23), 100–14 (nn. 46–9); see also V. O. Klyuchevsky, *Kurs russkoi istorii, lektsiya* XV, in *Sochineniya*, i (M., 1956), 261.

[23] *ZSL kratkoi*, 25–6. For the text of Yaroslav's Church Statute, in its 'short' and 'expanded' redactions, see *Pamyatniki russkogo prava*, i, ed. A. A. Zimin (M., 1952), 259–62, 265–72. Compare particularly the following chapters from the 'short' redaction of the *Judicial Law* with those from the two redactions of Yaroslav's Church Statute:

determined.[24] But the similarity between the two documents suggests that the *Judicial Law* reflects, as Zimin has suggested regarding the Church Statute, the 'attempt of the church to obtain effective results in its struggle against the vestiges of paganism, first of all in family and marriage relations', and to use the support of secular authority in combating those who violated the rules of morality.[25]

Most significantly, the 'short' redaction is linked with the efforts under way in Russia in the late thirteenth century to restore the cultural foundations of the past in the wake of the Mongol invasion. At a church council held in 1274 Metropolitan Kirill lamented that the church was not living in accordance with God's ordinances and that the rule of the pagan Tatars had resulted from this neglect. And he put much of the blame for the breakdown within the church upon the fact that the rules of the apostles and church fathers were not readily available in an intelligible Slavonic.[26] The council undertook, therefore, as part of its programme to restore ecclesiastical law, the compilation of a Russian *Kormchaya kniga*, a collection of church rules and civil laws that would be the equivalent of a *Nomocanon*.[27]

Metropolitan Kirill had received a copy of a Slavonic *Kormchaya* from Bulgaria. To the rules of the apostles, church fathers, and emperors as set forth in that document, the council added those rules which had developed and been used in Kiev and Novgorod. This compilation was subsequenly copied, recopied, and supplemented in different centres in an effort to gather together all juridical documents in use in Russia at the time, whether translated or of Russian origin. The earliest surviving text of the 'short' redaction of the *Judicial Law* appeared in the *Kormchaya* compiled in Novgorod.[28] And the text would be incorporated into manuscripts of other compilations of the *Kormchaya*.

'Short' Judicial Law	'Short' Church Statute	'Expanded' Church Statute
7	15	18
8	9	11
14	12	14
15	7	8
17	10	12 and 46
33		53

[24] For a detailed analysis of the church statutes of Vladimir and Yaroslav, in which the author removes the layers of later accretions to reach a hypothetical protograph of each text, see the recent study by Shchapov, *Knyazheskie ustavy* (n. 20); Shchapov also suggests (p. 78) that two articles, covering robbery of churches and graves, were inserted into Vladimir's Church Statute from a text 'close' to the 'short' redaction of the *Judicial Law*.

[25] Zimin, *Pamyatniki russkogo prava*, i, 257.

[26] For the text of the 'Pravilo Kirilla mitropolita', see *Russkaya istoricheskaya biblioteka, izdavaemaya Imp. Arkheograficheskoyu kommissieyu*, vi, pt. 1 (Spb., 1908), cols. 83–102.

[27] For the details of this process of Russian legal revival, see M. N. Tikhomirov, 'Vossozdanie russkoi pis'mennoi traditsii v pervye desyatiletiya tatarskogo iga', *Vestnik mirovoi kul'tury*, 1957 no. 3, pp. 3–13.

[28] For the textual history, see Tikhomirov, op. cit. (n. 27), 7–8, *ZSL kratkoi* (n. 1), 8–11, and Shchapov, op. cit. (n. 15), 295–301.

At approximately the same time that compilation of the Russian *Korm-chaya kniga* was going on, work was progressing on other juridical compilations as part of the same impulse toward recovering and making available the sources of Russian law. These collections of advice to judges and various juridical documents, which came to be known as the *Merilo pravednoe*, the 'Just Measure' or 'Scales of Justice', also date from the end of the thirteenth century. The text of the *Judicial Law* is included in some of these works. While apparently intended originally as a guide for civil judges, compilations with this title also came to be widespread among the upper clergy.[29]

This process of legal recovery resulted in the appearance not only of a large number of copies of the 'short' redaction of the *Judicial Law*, but of a second version of the code, the 'expanded' redaction. With a few exceptions historians neglected this second version until Tikhomirov published the variant texts, along with photographic reproductions of the manuscripts in 1961.[30] The oldest surviving copy of the 'expanded' redaction, the 'Pushkin' recension, is found in a manuscript compilation that palaeographic evidence indicates as originating in Novgorod in the mid fourteenth century.[31] A second recension, the 'Archaeographic', was included as part of the Novgorod First Chronicle, later recension. The Archaeographic Commission copy of the Novgorod First Chronicle has been dated by watermarks and handwriting as mid-fifteenth-century.[32] But textual analysis has led Tikhomirov to suggest the hypothesis that the protograph of the 'expanded' redaction dates from the late thirteenth century, approximately the same time as the work on the other legal compilations and handbooks.[33]

Yet there are striking differences between the two versions of the *Judicial Law*. Although all the chapters in the 'short' redaction are included in the 'expanded' version, textual analysis indicates that the compiler also consulted a text of the Byzantine *Ecloga*, probably a Slavonic translation taken from a *Kormchaya kniga*.[34] More important, the text has been expanded from

[29] On the *Merilo pravednoe*, see N. V. Kalachov, 'Merilo pravednoe', *Arkhiv istoriko-yuridicheskikh svedenii, otnosyashchikhsya k Rossii*, I, section 3 (Spb., 1876), 29–42; *Merilo pravednoe po rukopisi XIV veka*, ed. M. N. Tikhomirov (M., 1961), photographic reproduction of *Judicial Law* text on pp. 252–62; *ZSL kratkoi*, 14–18; Tikhomirov, op. cit. (n. 27), 9–10.

[30] M. N. Tikhomirov, *ed.*, *Zakon sudnyi lyudem prostrannoi i svodnoi redaktsii* (M., 1961). This volume also includes texts of a third version of the *Judicial Law*, the so-called 'concordance' redaction. This third redaction will not be dealt with here, since it represents a later attempt to produce a unified text of the *Judicial Law* by combining the two earlier redactions, with no change in the basic contents of the code.

[31] For a description of the manuscript, see *ZSL prostrannoi*, 6–9; for the text of the 'Pushkin' recension, see 33–43, 175–214.

[32] For a description of the manuscript, see *ZSL prostrannoi*, 10–12; for the text of the 'Archaeographic' recension, see 44–78, 215–39. On both recensions, see also M. N. Tikhomirov, *Issledovanie o Russkoi Pravde* (M., 1941), 143–55.

[33] *ZSL prostrannoi*, 8–9.

[34] Compare, for example, the article 'O chernorizchi' of the 'expanded' redaction (*ZSL prostrannoi*, 34) with ch. 5 of the 'short' version. In its revised form, the provision clearly refers to the punishment for anyone who fornicates with a nun, as does its model in the *Ecloga*, ch. 17, article 23; the text of the 'short' redaction, however, may be read as stating the punishment for a licentious monk. Suvorov demonstrated that the 'expanded' text also shows clear copying from the 'short' version (op. cit. (n. 2), 135–6, 139). For other vestiges of the 'short' redaction wording in the 'expanded' text, see *ZSL prostrannoi*, 15.

the 30-odd chapters in the 'short' redaction to 85 or more chapters.[35] These additional chapters include provisions concerning ecclesiastical discipline (ch. 44, 46, 56, 61, 66), crimes of various sorts (ch. 45, 47, 49, 52, 58, 63), agricultural matters and animals (ch. 48, 51, 55), testimony and false accusation (ch. 54, 57, 64, 65), and a series of regulations governing testamentary arrangements, witnesses to wills, and relations between heirs and executors (ch. 80–5). Many are based on Greek sources—canons of the church or Byzantine legal codes such as the *Ecloga*, *Procheiron*, and Farmers' Law.[36] The language and procedural requirements of others suggest Russian origin.[37]

But nearly half of the new chapters are either direct translations from Exodus, Leviticus, or Deuteronomy, or are clearly influenced by the Old Testament.[38] In setting norms for punishment of offences, the text refers

[35] The precise number varies from one manuscript to another. In texts of the 'expanded' redaction, chapters are not numbered. In some instances the content has been rearranged— for example, the chapter 'O mrtvtsě' (ch. 29 of the earliest copy of the 'short' redaction, *ZSL kratkoi*, 39) appears at the end of the 'Pushkin' recension of the 'expanded' text (*ZSL prostrannoi*, 43), whereas in the 'Archaeographic' recension it appears in regular sequence among the chapters taken from the 'short' redaction (*ZSL prostrannoi*, 65). On other occasions a scribe has combined under one heading two or more passages which appear as separate chapters in another manuscript; for example, ch. 33 of the 'short' version, 'Concerning husband and wife', has been broken into five separate sections in the 'Pushkin' recension (*ZSL prostrannoi*, 37–8) and four in the 'Archaeographic' (*ZSL prostrannoi*, 66–7), and each scribe has omitted, to differing degrees, portions of the text found in the 'short' redaction. There are also a number of what we might call 'wandering' articles, articles of purely Russian origin, one or more of which were added to various manuscript copies of the 'expanded' text (see *ZSL prostrannoi*, 7, 12, 19–20). None of them are found in the text of the 'Pushkin' recension, but four appear at the end of the 'Archaeographic' text (*ZSL prostrannoi*, 77–8); for other texts with different combinations of these articles, see *ZSL prostrannoi*, 117, 149. These provisions, which concern such matters as damage to another's spear, payment for feeding of children, slavery in times of famine, and fines for injury to honour, apparently were added gradually to various copies of the *Judicial Law*, and, at least in one instance, we find one of these articles 'wandering' toward a text of the *Russkaya Pravda*. The article concerning a spear appears near the end of the 'expanded' redaction of the *Judicial Law* in the 'Archaeographic' recension (*ZSL prostrannoi*, 77), but is found in the 'Pushkin' recension immediately following a text of the 'expanded' *Russkaya Pravda* and preceding the first chapter of the 'expanded' text of the *Judicial Law* (*ZSL prostrannoi*, 7). On the relationship between these 'wandering' articles and the *Russkaya Pravda*, see Tikhomirov, op. cit. (n.32), 154–5, and N. Kalachov, *Predvaritel'nye yuridicheskie svedeniya dlya polnogo ob"yasneniya Russkoi Pravdy* (M., 1846), 148–9. With particular reference to the article on injured honour (*beschest'e*), see Klyuchevsky, op. cit. (n. 22), 263–4, and Shchapov, *Knyazheskie ustavy* (n. 20), 271. In the following discussion of the contents of the 'expanded' redaction chapters have been numbered according to the order in which they appear in the 'Pushkin' recension.

[36] *ZSL prostrannoi*, 13–21. Tikhomirov provides a number of illustrations showing how the compiler corrected the *Judicial Law* text on the basis of the *Procheiron* and other sources.

[37] *ZSL prostrannoi*, 17, 20–1.

[38] For identification of the sources of the majority of chapters in the 'expanded' redaction, see Saturník, op. cit. (n. 11), 143–64. For the selections from Mosaic law the compiler of the 'expanded' redaction probably drew upon a work entitled 'Izbranie iz Moiseevykh zakonov', a version of which was often included in compilations of juridical materials; see *ZSL kratkoi*, 10, 16–17, 19–20, and *ZSL prostrannoi*, 15–17. But Suvorov points out (op. cit. (n. 2), 155) that the compiler of the 'expanded' redaction included several articles from Mosaic law which are not found in the Greek or other Slavonic extracts, probably borrowing them directly from the Bible.

directly to Moses and his prescription of 'an eye for an eye' (ch. 53, 69)—a principle repudiated in the New Testament. The code incorporates the Old Testament prohibitions on unnatural sex acts (ch. 59, 62, 66), and stresses the necessity for restitution in cases of lost, destroyed, or stolen property (ch. 50, 71–3, 78), for proper moral treatment of others (ch. 42, 60, 74–5, 78), and for just legal procedures (ch. 43, 65, 67–70, 73, 75, 77, 79). This reliance on Mosaic law as a major source for the additional material may reflect, as Suvorov has argued, Western influence and a belief in the greater authority of God-given law.[39] My own conclusion, however, is that the 'expanded' redaction's drawing upon the Old Testament, in apparent rejection of the New Testament's insistence that Mosaic law had been superseded, indicates a link between the 'expanded' redaction and the so-called Strigol'nik heresy that appeared in Novgorod about the middle of the fourteenth century.[40]

Unfortunately little is known about the views of the Strigol'niki, since our only information comes from materials written by their opponents. But it would appear that the Strigol'niki condemned priests for living in an improper manner, complained about simony in the church and excessive church fees, and objected that free men were being enslaved and sold for the sake of profit.[41] The views of the Strigol'niki on morality and proper conduct are paralleled in the principles of the 'expanded' redaction of the *Judicial Law*. The 'expanded' redaction puts heavy emphasis on sexual morality, prohibits the enslavement or sale of free persons, proscribes excessive fees for ordination and church functions, lays down rules governing the proper conduct of the clergy, and provides for additional penalties in cases of perjured testimony and false accusation. And most strikingly, the selections from Mosaic law emphasize the necessity of an upright life, based upon a stern moral code and concern for the welfare of others: lost property shall be returned and restitution made for anything stolen or damaged; labour shall be done honestly; no one shall profit at another's expense; decisions shall not be made unjustly or in return for bribes; infringement of the law shall be punished without mercy, as Moses prescribed.

Further support for a link between the new version of the *Judicial Law* and the Strigol'niki is found in chapter 54 of the 'expanded' redaction, entitled 'Concerning a heretic'. Rather than condemning heretics, prescribing punishment, or providing for investigation of charges, the chapter is directed against those who accuse others of heresy. True to the Mosaic principle anyone who brings a false charge of heresy in court is to receive the same punishment as the alleged heretic would have been given. And anyone who calls another a heretic—presumably out of court—is to be struck with a knife.[42] Since there is no such provision in the 'short' redaction, this addition

---

[39] Suvorov, op. cit. (n. 2), 149, 152, 155.

[40] On the origins of the heresy at this time, see N. A. Kazakova and Ya. S. Lur'e, *Antifeodal'nye ereticheskie dvizheniya na Rusi XIV—nachala XVI veka* (M.–L., 1955), 35.

[41] On the Strigol'niki, see ibid. 34–73; I. U. Budovnits, *Russkaya publitsistika XVI veka* (M.–L., 1947), 43–7; A. I. Klibanov, *Reformatsionnye dvizheniya v Rossii v XIV—pervoi polovine XVI vv.* (M., 1960), 118–66.

[42] Suvorov discusses the meaning of the chapter, but offers no comment on its origin or significance (op. cit. (n. 2), 142).

suggests a receptivity to—or at least a tolerance for—unorthodox views, such as those associated first with the Strigol'niki and then with the Judaizers, in early fourteenth-century Novgorod society.

If this hypothesis is correct, the efforts at restoring a solid legal foundation for Russian society after the disaster of the Mongol–Tartar invasion may have succeeded too well, at least in this one area, to suit the original sponsors of the programme. As a part of this activity, Mosaic law had taken firm root in Novgorod. Thus, the ground had been prepared for the struggles that would wrack the Russian church in the years that lay ahead.

The Logic of Madness:
Gogol´'s *Zapiski sumasshedshego*

By R. A. PEACE

WRITING in 1835 Belinsky described *Zapiski sumasshedshego* as: 'this psycho-logical case history, depicted in poetic form, which is remarkable for its truth and its profundity . . .'.[1] It is the aim of the present essay to explore this view, and to show that the poetic flights of Poprishchin's fancy are no mere exercise in the grotesque, but have their own psychological necessity, their own inner logic, and that the story may indeed be read as a case history 'remarkable for its truth and its profundity'.

The opening sentence establishes the sense of a 'history'—of a record in time of something abnormal:

Октября 3
Сегодняшнего дня случилось необыкновенное приключение.
(193)[2]

Yet the events which are related immediately after this arresting opening are in quite another key. Our hero has overslept and does not feel like going to the office because he knows what reception will await him from the head of his section:

«Что это у тебя, братец, в голове всегда ералаш такой? Ты иной раз метаешься как угорелый, дело подчас так спутаешь, что сам сатана не разберет, в титуле поставишь маленькую букву, не выставишь ни числа, ни номера». (193)

Thus from the very first page the record of the unusual event is juxtaposed with the hero's inadequacy at work. This in itself is indicative.

To justify himself against this criticism, he claims that the head of section is merely envious of him for his occasional job of sharpening pens in the director's study. But as the diary unfolds it seems more likely that Poprishchin has been given this more menial task because of his unreliability as a copying clerk, and that it is not his immediate superior who feels envy of him, but rather the other way round: it is Poprishchin himself who envies his superiors, particularly the life of the director, on whom he is sent to wait as a sort of office-boy. Thus from the outset, Poprishchin falls back on two psychological defences against the real world: the inversion of his true status (i.e. inadequacy becomes privilege) and the projection of his own psychology on to a third person (i.e. his *own* envy becomes that of the head of section). These two devices are to assume growing importance as the story progresses. Poprishchin's thoughts proceed by association, and are often unintentionally

---

[1] V. G. Belinsky, *Polnoe sobranie sochinenii*, i (M., 1953), 297.
[2] All page references are to the text in N. V. Gogol´, *Polnoe sobranie sochinenii*, iii (M., 1937). Hereafter this edition is referred to as *PSS*.

revealing. He strives to assert his independence of the office by claiming that he would not go there at all today if he did not need an advance on his salary. Yet his very next words reveal that he knows that he has no hope of receiving such an advance. This admission leads him not only to strong personal criticism of the office treasurer, but also to complain about the poor remuneration his job brings compared with provincial offices (where bribes are possible). So if he is not working for money—he must be working for honour:

> Правда, у нас зато служба благородная, чистота во всем такая, какой вовеки не видеть губернскому правлению: столы из красного дерева, и все начальники на *bbl*. Да, признаюсь, если бы не благородство службы, я бы давно оставил департамент. (194)

The consciousness of being noble is central to Poprishchin's preoccupation with his own status, and it is significant that the first mention of 'nobility' is connected with his work in the civil service; for Poprishchin is a nobleman merely by virtue of the civil service rank he holds—that of titular councillor. Yet it is a rather ambiguous nobility; for 'titular councillor' was a natural sticking place in the Table of Ranks, as it only conferred nobility on the holder, and promotion into the next grade was essential for such nobility to become hereditary.

Walking reluctantly to the office through the rain, he comments that there is nobody on the street (nobody, of course, apart from members of the lower orders: peasant women, merchants and coach drivers):

> Из благородных только наш брат чиновник плелся. Я увидел его на перекрестке. Я, как увидел его, тотчас сказал себе: «Эге! нет, голубчик, ты не в департамент идешь, ты спешишь вон за тою, что бежит впереди, и глядишь на ее ножки».[3] Что это за бестия наш брат чиновник! Ей-богу, не уступит никакому офицеру: пройди какая-нибудь в шляпке, непременно зацепит. (194)

There is an obvious contradiction between the way this figure is perceived and the way he is then interpreted. On the one hand the civil servant is 'trudging' (reluctantly to the office?) and on the other he is 'hurrying' after a woman (cf. the verbs плелся and спешишь), and it is not difficult to see in this figure another of Poprishchin's 'projections'. The term 'our brother civil servant' (наш брат чиновник) is indeed a formula of dissociative self-identification which allows Poprishchin both to be, and not to be, the other person. In Poprishchin's eyes the 'brother at the cross roads' is, in the first place, noble; in the second place, unlike Poprishchin himself, he is showing his defiance of the department, and moreover is doing so in such a way as to reveal that he is not the inferior of any officer (true social status and nobility).[4]

---

[3] The notebook version had: 'что приподняла немного свое платье и показала в мгнове[ние?] икры свои' (*PSS*, iii, 554).

[4] Ranks in the civil service paralleled military ones, but, in the eyes of many, military rank had more prestige. Thus Poprishchin counters the criticism that he is a nonentity by claiming that he is capable of becoming a colonel (ibid. 198). The director (the man he really envies) always has his rank given as 'general'. In *Nos* Kovalev, a civil servant of the 8th grade, always refers to himself as 'major'.

But unfortunately at this point reality breaks in:

> Когда я думал это, увидел подъехавшую карету к магазину, мимо которого я проходил. Я сейчас узнал ее: это была карета нашего директора. «Но ему незачем в магазин, я подумал: верно, это его дочка». Я прижался к стенке. (194)

Thus the dashing way of the civil-service fraternity with women (as a mark of social status) is immediately given the lie by Poprishchin's despair:

> Господи, боже мой! пропал я, пропал совсем.

He makes every effort not to be seen and the director's daughter sweeps past him into the shop leaving him unnoticed on the wet pavement. But he is not alone in this situation:

> Собачонка ее, не успевши вскочить в дверь магазина, осталась на улице. (194–5)

A comparison of his lot to that of the dog of the director's daughter is too near the truth:[5] a 'projection' of a completely different order takes place— an hallucination in which the dog is clearly addressed by another dog which is also on the street. This is the 'unusual adventure' the reader was promised in the opening sentence. Poprishchin's failure is not merely that he has been unable to live up to his idealized, dashing 'brother civil servant': he has actually shrunk from all personal contact with the woman who means most to him. Not surprisingly the dogs' brief conversation is entirely devoted to a failure to communicate, but here the blame lies squarely with the dog of the director's daughter:

«Грех тебе, Меджи!» says the other dog Fidèle (the significance of this name will be apparent). But Medzhi justifies herself:

> Нет, Фидель, ты напрасно думаешь, . . . я была, ав! ав! я была, ав, ав, ав! очень больна». (195)

Medzhi's jerky delivery seems to suggest an improvised excuse, but she goes on to suggest yet another reason:

> «Я писала к тебе, Фидель; верно, Полкан не принес письма моего!» (ibid.)

---

[5] 'The significance of the dogs in *Zapiski sumasšedšego* is great: in their implied inter-changeability with men they underline Poprishchin's (man's) essential animalness and his inability to rise from the mire of reality into a better and more meaningful world.' S. Juran, '*Zapiski sumasšedšego*: Some insights into Gogol''s world', *The Slavic and East European Journal*, N.S., v (xix) (1961), 331.

Throughout *Zapiski sumasshedshego* Gogol' draws much of his imagery from the animal kingdom. Thus Sofi is first introduced as a bird: '. . . она выпорхнула из кареты, как птичка' (*PSS*, iii, 194). On her second appearance she enters her father's office in a dress as white as a swan and her voice is that of a canary (ibid. 196). Bird imagery is also used to convey negative attributes. The head of section is a 'heron' (193), and a certain Bobov is likened to a stork (204). Other animals are also referred to. Apart from the usual references to pigs (i.e. civil servants, 199) and donkeys (i.e. tailors, 210), the most striking is the expression 'a tortoise in a sack' (204), referring to Poprishchin himself.

Thus there are valid excuses for a breakdown of communication, even among dogs.

Poprishchin decides to follow Fidèle to learn more about her. He seems concerned to give the route he follows quite precisely (i.e. names of streets, etc.).[6] Yet, notwithstanding this, there also appears to be something 'internal' about the whole exercise:

Пойду-ка я, *сказал я сам b себе,*[7] за этой собачонкою и узнаю, чтò она и чтò такое думает. (ibid.)

The same formula (сказал я сам в себе) is repeated when he recognizes the house in which Fidèle lives:

Этот дом я знаю, сказал я сам в себе. Это дом Зверкова. (195–6)

The house of Zverkov was an actual building in St. Petersburg. Moreover, it had overtones of self-identification for the author himself; for Gogol' had lived there as an indigent civil servant.[8] But this aside, the name itself suggests *zver'*—'animal', and its inhabitants live like animals, especially the civil servants:

Эка машина! Какого в нем народа не живет: сколько кухарок, сколько поляков! а нашей братьи чиновников, как собак, один на другом сидит. Там есть и у меня один приятель, который хорошо играет на трубе. (196)

Thus not only is the house of Zverkov the home of a dog (Fidèle) but 'our brother civil servants' also live there 'like dogs'.[9] 'Our brother civil servants' (наша братья чиновники) is, of course, another of Poprishchin's dissociative formulae of self-identification, and its force here seems to be strengthened by his claim to have a friend amongst them (the only one of whom we hear).

Fidèle's owners live on the fourth floor (i.e. the poorest part of a poor house). The social status of Fidèle is thus established and Poprishchin feels no need to go further, in spite of his earlier stated objective of finding out also what she thought. He is now reassured that the social gulf, which divides poor civil servants from the daughters of directors, can be bridged, if only by their canine substitutes, and he makes a note, in case the need to resort to this fiction should arise again:

Хорошо, подумал я: теперь не пойду, а замечу место и при первом случае не премину воспользоваться. (ibid.)

[6] Gogol' is similarly precise about location in the ghost sequence at the end of *Shinel'* (*PSS*, iii, 169–74), whereas earlier in the story when the living Akaky Akakievich had walked the streets of St. Petersburg the narrator had proved incapable of giving any such information (ibid. 158). See my article, 'Gogolj i psihološki realizam: "Šinjel" ', *Filološki pregled*, i–ii (Belgrade, 1975), 38.
[7] My italics. This is, in fact, the version of the notebooks. See *PSS*, iii, 555, 559.
[8] Ibid. 703.
[9] Dogs and 'those who write' are thus connected. Cf. the saying: 'Писал писачка и имя его собачка', quoted by Gogol' himself in *Vybrannye mesta iz perepiski s druz'yami* (*PSS*, viii, 272).

The next entry is for the following day (4 October). The events described are quite ordinary and serve to lull the reader's suspicions about Poprishchin's sanity, yet, at the same time, they reveal the inner tensions brought about by his position in the office.

It is a day when he works in the director's study, and so, in marked contrast to the day before, he purposely comes early. The director has made a great impression on him:

> Весь кабинет его уставлен шкафами с книгами. Я читал название некоторых: всё ученость, такая ученость, что нашему брату и приступа нет: всё или на французском, или на немецком. А посмотреть в лицо ему: фу, какая важность сияет в глазах! Я еще никогда не слышал, чтобы он сказал лишнее слово. Только разве когда подашь бумаги, спросит: «Каково на дворе?»—«Сыро, ваше превосходительство!» Да, не нашему брату чета! Государственный человек (ibid.)

We can see that to soften the blow, when comparing himself to the director, Poprishchin again resorts to his formula of dissociative self-identification (наш брат). He believes that the director likes him, and he, for his part, tries to ape him. So, immediately after his remarks on the foreign tomes of the 'statesman's' library, Poprishchin himself proclaims an interest in foreign affairs, as reported in *Severnaya pchela*:

> Читал «Пчелку». Эка глупый народ французы! Ну, чего хотят они? Взял бы, ей-богу, их всех, да и перепорол розгами! (ibid).

It is this ill-informed concern for foreign politics, which will later grow into the central obsession of his madness.

The other item which catches his attention in *Severnaya pchela* (a description of a ball by a landowner from Kursk) requires him to cope with a topic he has just vetoed—the life of Sofi:

> Если бы и дочка . . . эх, канальство! . . . Ничего, ничего, молчание! (ibid).

Poprishchin's love for the director's daughter is both comic and tragic, but it is also mixed in another way: it has elements of the genuine erotic, as when later he thinks about her in her boudoir, having just risen from bed and pulling on her white stockings. Nevertheless, more deeply felt than this is his desire to possess her for her status, or alternatively (as his mixed emotions are not without their element of masochism) to be punished by such a torturingly inaccessible yet 'powerful' figure. Thus, when he now suddenly finds himself alone in the room with her the effect on Poprishchin is excruciating:

> «Ваше превосходительство, хотел я было сказать, не прикажите казнить, а если уже хотите казнить, то казните вашею генеральскою ручкою». (196–7)

When shortly afterwards she drops her handkerchief and he rushes to pick it up, the fragrance it exudes is not sexual allurement but the attraction of status:

амбра, совершенная амбра! так и дышит от него генеральством. (197)

During this brief encounter with the director's daughter, Poprishchin is completely tongue-tied and cuts a pathetically comic figure.

His day ends with another attempt to ape what he takes to be the culture of his betters: he copies out some third-rate love poetry, which he mistakenly thinks is Pushkin. Its sentiments he obviously associates with Sofi, for he spends the rest of the evening hanging about outside her door.

After the first two consecutive entries, there is a gap of thirty-three days.[10] Criticism of Poprishchin by his head of section had figured prominently in the first entry and it is another attack from this source which seems to precipitate the next series of entries:

Разбесил начальник отделения. Когда я пришел в департамент, он подозвал меня к себе и начал мне говорить так: «Ну, скажи пожалуйста, что ты делаешь?»—«Как что? Я ничего не делаю», отвечал я.—«Ну, размысли хорошенько! ведь тебе уже за сорок лет—пора бы ума набраться. Что ты воображаешь себе? Ты думаешь, я не знаю всех твоих проказ? Ведь ты волочишься за директорскою дочерью! Ну, посмотри на себя, подумай только, что ты? ведь ты нуль, более ничего. Ведь у тебя нет ни гроша за душою. Взгляни хоть в зеркало на свое лицо, куды тебе думать о том!» (197–8)

This is devastating criticism of Poprishchin. He is attacked where he is most vulnerable, and his only defence is to launch a counter-attack through his diary, ridiculing in his turn the face, general appearance and social pretensions of his detractor:

Велика важность надворный советник! вывесил золотую цепочку к часам, заказывает сапоги по тридцати рублей—да чорт его побери! Я разве из каких-нибудь разночинцев, из портных или из унтер-офицерских детей? Я дворянин. Что ж, и я могу дослужиться. Мне еще сорок два года—время такое, в которое, по-настоящему, только что начинается служба. (198)

Poprishchin's tragedy is that his much vaunted status as a nobleman is intimately connected with his post in the civil service, and far from being able to advance this position through service (дослужиться: he talks here of becoming a colonel or even something higher), he finds his present duties are really beyond him, and in this context his name (поприще—'career') has a very ironic ring.

Two days later he consoles himself at the theatre watching a vaudeville in which criticism is directed at other, lower, strata of society. Moreover, in

[10] Surprisingly, this gap is overlooked by G. A. Gukovsky; see his *Realizm Gogolya* (M.–L., 1959), 302. It is usual in English to call the work a 'diary', but the Russian title is *Zapiski* . . . ('notes'); the work is, therefore, not a day to day record, but made up of erratic entries.

the mere fact that he goes to the theatre, he sees his cultural superiority over his fellow civil servants, and here the dissociative formula of self-identification is given a different emphasis:

> Как только грош заведется в кармане—никак не утерпишь не пойти. А вот из нашей братьи чиновников есть такие свиньи: решительно не пойдет, мужик, в театр; разве уже дашь ему билет даром. (198–9)

Nevertheless the voice of one of the actresses reminds him of Sofi, and once more he is forced to bottle up his feelings—with the prohibition 'Молчание!'

The following day apparently passes without incident, but in the entry which follows two days later he has reached a point of crisis. After having been told so categorically by the head of his section that he is a nonentity, he is now once more confronted with the importance of the director and all the significance he represents:

> У! должен быть голова! Всё молчит, а в голове, я думаю, всё обсуживает. Желалось бы мне узнать, о чем он больше всего думает; что такое затевается в этой голове. (199)

The fact that Poprishchin identifies the director's position and authority with the quality of silence only reinforces his own difficulties in communication; for in aping the director he places the veto of silence on his own most deeply felt emotions. As we have seen, he cannot raise the subject of the director's daughter, even with himself, without immediately invoking that word, of which her father would, no doubt, approve: 'Молчание!' The result is that like the director himself (or at least as Poprishchin imagines him) everything goes on within his own head—the one outlet is his erratic jotting in the 'notes'. Yet the situation is impossible: he must at all costs escape from his own nonentity into the world of significance and status, or, at the very least, see this world at first hand:

> Хотелось бы мне рассмотреть поближе жизнь этих господ, все эти экивоки и придворные штуки—как они, что́ они делают в своем кругу—вот что бы мне хотелось узнать! (ibid.)

As is to be expected, his efforts to learn something from the director himself are inhibited by the laws of 'Молчание'.

> Я думал несколько раз завести разговор с его превосходи-тельством, только, чорт возьми, никак не ˙слушается язык: скажешь только, холодно или тепло на дворе, а больше решительно ничего не выговоришь. (ibid.)

He has an urge to pry into the inner recesses of their private life:

> Хотелось бы мне заглянуть в гостиную, куда видишь только иногда отворенную дверь, за гостиною еще в одну комнату. Эх, какое богатое убранство! Какие зеркала и фарфоры! Хотелось бы заглянуть туда, на ту половину, где ее превосходительство, вот куда хотелось бы мне! в будуар: как там стоят все эти баночки, скляночки, цветы такие, что и дохнуть на них страшно; как лежит там разбросанное ее платье, больше похожее на воздух, чем на

платье. Хотелось бы заглянуть в спальню . . . там-то, я думаю, чудеса, там-то, я думаю, рай, какого и на небесах нет. Посмотреть бы ту скамеечку, на которую она становит, вставая с постели, свою ножку, как надевается на эту ножку белый, как снег, чулочек . . . (199–200)

Predictably the inevitable veto ends further speculation:

ай! ай! ай! ничего, ничего . . . молчание.

But it is precisely here at this point of impasse that inspiration suddenly seizes him:

Сегодня, однако ж, меня как бы светом озарило: я вспомнил тот разговор двух собачонок, который слышал я на Невском проспекте. «Хорошо,—подумал я сам в себе [again the more internal formula—R.A.P.]: я теперь узнаю всё». (200)

The promise he had made to himself when first discovering where Fidèle lived is now activated: he must resort to the dogs once more in order to gain that entrée into the private life of the director and his daughter which he so desires, but which, in the real world, is so impossible. At first he tries talking to Medzhi, but receives no reply. However, the fact that direct communication between him and the dog is not possible he merely sees as a mark of the qualities he so admires in her master:

Я давно подозревал, что собака гораздо умнее человека; я даже был уверен, что она может говорить, но что в ней есть только какое-то упрямство. Она чрезвычайный политик: всё замечает, все шаги человека. (ibid.)

It is the communication of dog with dog which will tell him all he needs to know. The following afternoon he calls at the apartment of Fidèle to collect Medzhi's letters:

Эти письма мне всё откроют. Собаки народ умный, они знают все политические отношения, и потому верно там будет всё: портрет и все дела этого мужа. Там будет что-нибудь и о той, которая . . . ничего, молчание! (201)

When he gets a chance to examine the letters next day (13 November) his first concern seems to be with form:

А ну, посмотрим: письмо довольно четкое. Однакоже в почерке всё есть как будто что-то собачье. (ibid.)

For Poprishchin handwriting is intimately connected with status. On overhearing the dogs' conversation in the first place, he had been less surprised by their ability to speak than by their apparent ability to write:

Да чтоб я не получил жалованья! Я еще в жизни не слыхивал, чтобы собака могла писать. Правильно писать может только дворянин. Оно конечно, некоторые и купчики-конторщики и даже крепостной народ пописывает иногда; но их писание большею частью механическое: ни запятых, ни точек, ни слога. (195)

This view of the art of writing as a specific class attribute (правильно писать может только дворянин) goes to the heart of Poprishchin's anxiety. He is 'noble' because of his position in the civil service hierarchy, and, as he is only a copying clerk, it is a position he holds by virtue of his ability to write. Yet the technical and stylistic faults, which he sees as a mark of the lower orders, are no worse than those for which he himself has been criticized and it is indicative that his surprise at the dogs' ability to write should be prefaced by the oath:

'да чтоб я не получил жалованья!'[11]

Nevertheless Medzhi is the communicator of the secrets of the director's household—she is the scribe of values to which he aspires and as such her writing skill must be beyond reproach. After reading the first paragraph of her letter Poprishchin's earlier doubts are assuaged:

Письмо писано очень правильно.[12] Пунктуация и даже буква ѣ везде на своем месте. Да эдак просто не напишет и наш начальник отделения, хотя он и толкует, что где-то учился в университете. (202)

The dog's handwriting, in establishing her social position, is at the same time also a reproach to Poprishchin's greatest critic, and if the form of the letter reveals Medzhi's social superiority, its content underlines the lower social status of the recipient:

Милая Фидель! я всё не могу привыкнуть к твоему мещанскому имени. Как будто бы уже не могли дать тебе лучшего? Фидель, Роза—какой пошлый тон, однакож, всё это в сторону. Я очень рада, что мы вздумали писать друг к другу. (201)

On his way to collect the letters Poprishchin had been acutely aware of the low social standing of the area where Fidèle lives, with its smells, its smoke and its grime:

Человеку благородному решительно невозможно здесь прогуливаться.

These are impressions which appear to have escaped him when he first followed Fidèle home, and the dog seems now to live in an even worse part of the building, the fifth floor rather than the fourth.[13]

The need to stress the lowly social origins of Fidèle is as important as the need to emphasize the good breeding of Medzhi; for the essential function of the dogs' letters is that they bridge a social gap which cannot be bridged in the real world. They are a fantasy about communication in which the formula of dissociative self-identification reaches its most sophisticated form: Poprishchin both *is* and *is not* Fidèle; Medzhi both *is* and *is not* Sofi. The device is an эκивок (i.e. *double entendre*) of Poprishchin's over-driven imagination, which

---

[11] The notebook version had the more usual expletive: 'чорт возьми' (*PSS*, iii, 555).
[12] Cf. the earlier statement: 'Правильно писать может только дворянин' (ibid. 195).
[13] Ibid. 196, 200.

serves to answer the need for the 'эквивоки и придворные штуки' of the life of those he so envies.

The pleasures of communication are the very next thought expressed by Medzhi in her letter:

Мне кажется, что разделять мысли, чувства и впечатления с другим есть одно из первых благ на свете. (202)

This is an auspicious start, but at the first mention of Sofi's name Poprishchin has his usual reaction:

Ай, ай! . . . ничего, ничего. Молчание! (ibid.)

The subject of Sofi thus being vetoed, the direction the dog's letter now takes is not at all to his liking—it is all about dogs' food. In annoyance Poprishchin has to turn to another page before he can find anything relevant: Medzhi begins to discuss her master. This is not a subject to veto:

А! вот наконец! Да; я знал: у них политический взгляд на все предметы. Посмотрим, чтò папа . . . (ibid.)

The dog's opening words on the director could just as well be a description of Poprishchin himself:

. . . очень странный человек. Он больше молчит. Говорит очень редко; но неделю назад беспрестанно говорил сам с собою: «Получу или не получу?» Возьмет в одну руку бумажку, другую сложит пустую и говорит: «Получу или не получу?» Один раз он обратился и ко мне с вопросом: «Как ты думаешь, Меджи? получу или не получу?» (ibid.)

The reason for the director's odd behaviour is much the same as that which lies behind the eccentricities of Poprishchin himself—anxiety over his career. But for the director there is a happy outcome—he receives the decoration which he covets. For Poprishchin the possibility of self-identification is reassuring, yet there is a flaw: the dog for all its supposed political astuteness, treats its master's preferment as a thing of little consequence—it is merely a ribbon with no smell which tastes slightly salty:

Гм! Эта собачонка, мне кажется, уже слишком . . . чтобы ее не высекли! А! так он честолюбец! Это нужно взять к сведению. (203)

Having learned something about the director which he can recognize as his own, Poprishchin seems less nervous on the subject of Sofi. When her name comes up again, he hesitates but ultimately does not apply his veto:

А! ну, посмотрим, что Софи. Эх, канальство! . . . Ничего, ничего . . . будем продолжать. (ibid.)

He learns of Sofi's bad temper when dressing for a ball and of her return at six in the morning. Unlike the ambition of her father, there is nothing here with which Poprishchin can readily identify, but as usual the note of criticism is left to the dog:

Я никак не понимаю, ma chère, удовольствия ехать на бал. (ibid.)

This lack of 'canine' understanding has the same force as Poprishchin's earlier veto, for now, as on that previous occasion, the details of Sofi's life are suddenly swamped by the irritating subject of dogs' dinners.

The content of the letters is obviously unsatisfactory, but Poprishchin's reaction is to criticize the form:

> Чрезвычайно неровный слог. Тотчас видно, что не человек писал. Начнет так, как следует, а кончит собачиною. (ibid.)

'Stylistically' the next letter he picks up augurs even worse. Poprishchin at once complains of a fault (which, significantly, is one of his own)—the writer has not given a date. It is not surprising that a letter which reminds him of his own transgressions of form should in its content reveal more substantial vulnerability; for when Medzhi discusses her suitors, it is not difficult to see in one of them a canine parody of Poprishchin himself:

> Иной преаляповатый, дворняга,[14] глуп страшно, на лице написана глупость, преважно идет по улице и воображает, что он презнатная особа, думает, что так на него и заглядятся все. Ничуть. Я даже и внимания не обратила, так, как бы и не видала его. (ibid.)

There are echoes here of the meeting on the street in the first entry. But worse is to follow: for in the name Trésor, the dog who really appeals to Medzhi, there is a phonetic echo of another name, Teplov—the real suitor of Sofi (indeed Medzhi is to make the comparison explicit in her next letter). It is at the mention of Trésor that Poprishchin breaks off his reading:

> Тьфу, к чорту! . . . Экая дрянь! . . . И как можно наполнять письма эдакими глупостями. Мне подавайте человека! Я хочу видеть человека; я требую пищи, той, которая бы питала и услаждала мою душу; а вместо того эдакие пустяки . . . (204)

Poprishchin's plea to be a given a human being and food which will nourish and content his soul is a cry from the heart. Whenever, up to now, Sofi has figured in the letters as a real human being, some sort of veto has been imposed, by which food has been given instead—not the spiritual nourishment he craves, but dogs' dinners. In rejecting these offerings, he turns to a letter which projects Sofi and her suitors in terms of dogs. The implications of the content of this letter are disturbing, but Poprishchin's reaction is to criticize the form in which the unpalatable information is presented—he wants human beings instead of dogs.

As if in answer to his cry, the next letter does, in fact, restate the problem in terms of human beings. He reads now of Teplov's visit to Sofi, but Medzhi's attitude to this gentleman of the bedchamber is highly critical. Therefore Poprishchin still feels he has a straw at which to clutch:

> Мне самому кажется, здесь что-нибудь да не так. Не может быть, чтобы ее мог так обворожить камер-юнкер. (ibid.)

---

[14] 'The clumsy mongrel resembles the clerk, just as his title (*dvornjaga* 'mongrel') resembles Poprishchin's own (*dvorjanin* 'nobleman')'. R. F. Gustafson, 'The Suffering Usurper: Gogol's *Diary of a Madman*', *The Slavic and East European Journal*, ix (1965), 271.

But the letter continues:

> Мне кажется, если камер-юнкер нравится, то скоро будет нра-
> виться и тот чиновник, который сидит у папа́ в кабинете. Ах, ma
> chère, если бы ты знала, какой это урод. Совершенная черепа-
> ха в мешке . . .(ibid.)

Poprishchin is leading himself towards the truth by gentle stages, and at this
point he can still feel that the reference is unclear:

> Какой же бы это чиновник? . . . (ibid.)

What follows, however, leaves him in no doubt:

> Фамилия его престранная. Он всегда сидит и чинит перья.
> Волоса на голове его очень похожи на сено. Папа́ всегда посылает
> его вместо слуги . . . (205)

Poprishchin at last recognizes himself, and then comes the final thrust:

> Софи никак не может удержаться от смеха, когда глядит на него.
> (ibid.)

The dog's letters have been for Poprishchin a means of discovering the truth,
but it is a truth which, on one level, he knew all along: that his relationship
to the director is virtually one of a servant, that Sofi can scarcely refrain from
laughing in his presence—both these facts had been clearly hinted by
Poprishchin himself as early as the second entry in his notes (4 October).
Here he had recorded that Sofi almost smirked when he handed back her
handkerchief, and immediately after this he reveals that he feels himself to
be patronized by the director's servants when they offer him snuff and fail to
stand in his presence. He thus feels the need to assert that he is not one of
them:

> Да знаешь ли ты, глупый холоп, что я чиновник, я благородного
> происхождения. (197)

If the director had received a decoration, the whole department would
certainly have known about it. Moreover, given Poprishchin's interest in Sofi
and his hanging about outside her door, he must have had some inkling of
her visits to balls and the admirers who called on her.

Poprishchin does not need the dog's letters to tell him these facts. Rather
he needs them as a partial defence against them—a means of coming to terms
with the truth. The function of the letters is both to conceal and to reveal, for
Poprishchin at one and the same time wants to know and not to know. Such
a device is ultimately unsatisfactory, and his growing impatience with it
leads to the truth coming out in all its glaring unpleasantness.

Poprishchin's first reaction to the truth is to refute it:

> Врешь ты, проклятая собачонка! (205)

then to put the blame on the 'form'—the dog's style:

> Экой мерзкий язык! (ibid.)

and from this it is easy to make the jump to the conclusion that the great critic of his own written style is behind it all:

> Как будто я не знаю, что это дело зависти. Как будто я не знаю, чьи здесь штуки. Это штуки начальника отделения. Ведь поклялся же человек непримиримою ненавистию—и вот вредит да и вредит, на каждом шагу вредит. (ibid.)

Thus the letters which started out as a reproach to the head of section are now seen as having been inspired by him after all.

In spite of this, Poprishchin cannot refrain from taking a look at the final letter. From it he learns of the impending marriage of Sofi and the gentleman of the bedchamber. The social gulf which the fantastic letters of Medzhi to Fidèle promised to bridge now yawns before him in all its stark reality:

> Чорт возьми! я не могу более читать. . . . Всё или камер-юнкер, или генерал. Всё, что есть лучшего на свете, всё достается или камер-юнкерам, или генералам. Найдешь себе бедное богатство, думаешь достать его рукою,—срывает у тебя камер-юнкер или генерал. (ibid.)

There is now a new note of defiance: he does not need Sofi in order to gain status, nor even need to acquire status in order to gain Sofi: he wants status for revenge:

> Чорт побери! Желал бы я сам сделаться генералом, не для того, чтобы получить руку и прочее. Нет; хотел бы быть генералом для того только, чтобы увидеть, как они будут увиваться и делать все эти разные придворные штуки и экивоки, и потом сказать им, что я плюю на вас обоих. (ibid.)

The entry ends with Poprishchin tearing up the dog's letters: they have proved inadequate as a filter for harsh reality.

After the sequence of entries in November (separated by gaps of one or two days at the most) there is a much greater break of twenty days before the next entry (3 December). As previously the new spate of entries is occasioned by his having to face up to an unpleasant truth—Sofi is getting married to the gentleman of the bedchamber:

> Не может быть. Враки! Свадьбе не бывать!

The new-found note of social criticism takes on Shakespearian overtones:[15]

> Что ж из того, что он камер-юнкер. Ведь это больше ничего, кроме достоинство; не какая-нибудь вещь видимая, которую бы можно взять в руки. Ведь через то, что камер-юнкер, не прибавит-ся третий глаз на лбу. Ведь у него же нос не из золота сделан, а так же, как и у меня, как и у всякого; ведь он им нюхает, а не ест, чихает, а не кашляет. (205–6)

---

[15] Cf. Shylock's speech on being a Jew, *The Merchant of Venice*, III, i. See Gukovsky, op. cit. (n. 10), 313. Poprishchin's speech also recalls Falstaff's monologue on honour in *1 Henry IV*, V, i. When Belinsky spoke of the work as a 'psychological case history, depicted in poetic form, which is remarkable for its truth and profundity, worthy of the brush of Shakespeare' (loc. cit. (n. 1)), he most probably had in mind Shakespeare's 'poetic' depiction of madness in Ophelia.

Previously, when Medzhi, through her comments on the director's decoration had suggested the emptiness of rank and honours, Poprishchin had thought such ideas dangerous. Now the emptiness of what he envies is an idea which can be used as a defence, but it still cannot explain the existence of the social gulf:

> Я несколько раз уже хотел добраться, отчего происходят все эти разности. Отчего я титулярный советник и с какой стати я титулярный советник? (206)

By questioning his own identity he can, in fact, arrive at another solution to his problem:

> Может быть я какой-нибудь граф или генерал, а только так кажусь титулярным советником? Может быть я сам не знаю, кто я таков. Ведь сколько примеров по истории: какой-нибудь простой, не то уже чтобы дворянин, а просто какой-нибудь мещанин или даже крестьянин—и вдруг открывается, что он какой-нибудь вельможа, а иногда даже и государь. Когда из мужика да иногда выходит эдакое, что же из дворянина может выйти? (ibid.)

With true madman's logic Poprishchin has prepared his position for the next stage in his fight against nonentity—the total inversion of his status.

Two days later he finds food for thought in the newspaper accounts of what is happening in Spain:

> чины находятся в затруднительном положении о избрании наследника и от того происходят возмущения. (ibid.)

The confusion seems to mirror his own inner state, and his own difficulties over ranks.[16] In his next entry, three days later (8 December), his thoughts prevent him from going to the office, and in his continued search for spiritual food he seems to be neglecting earthly sustenance:[17]

> Мавра замечала мне, что я за столом был чрезвычайно развлечен. И точно, я две тарелки, кажется, в рассеянности бросил на пол, которые тут же расшиблись. После обеда ходил под горы. Ничего поучительного не мог извлечь. Большею частию лежал на кровати и рассуждал о делах Испании. (207)

The next entry opens on a note of *Eureka*!

> Сегодняшний день—есть день величайшего торжества! В Испании есть король. (ibid.)

To mark this momentous occasion, Poprishchin for the first time includes the year in his date heading—but it is one appropriate to such an event: the

---

[16] The phrase 'чины находятся' was not in the draft version (*PSS*, iii, 565) and here too Poprishchin's nonentity was directly linked to his rank ('Ведь ты нуль. Ты—титулярный советник', ibid. 557).

[17] On his way to collect the letters from Fidèle he complained that he could not bear cabbage (ibid. 200).

doubly chiliastic year 2000. The month, too, suffers from similar illusions of grandeur—it is recorded as 43 April. This entry marks Poprishchin's final loss of all grip on reality. From now on the dates will get more and more nonsensical, until, with the final entry, they end in the greatest confusion of all.[18] Dates, which as a copying clerk, he frequently omitted from documents, now, as the King of Spain, he sets down with hyperbole and panache.

Poprishchin has finally found a delusion which makes him invulnerable to the inroads of reality. The formula of dissociative self-identification to which he had resorted in the device of the dogs was unsatisfactory—it was too ambiguous. Now what he has found is unequivocal self-identification with the power and prestige of a figure above gentlemen of the bedchamber and generals.

In many ways the new delusion has much in common with the old. It is a reflection of events in a far-away country about which he reads in the newspaper, much as earlier he had come to terms with the fact that dogs could talk by support from these same two sources:

> Говорят, в Англии выплыла рыба, которая сказала два слова на таком странном языке, что ученые уже три года стараются определить и еще до сих пор ничего не открыли. Я читал тоже в газетах о двух коровах, которые пришли в лавку и спросили себе фунт чаю. (195)[19]

The realization that he is the King of Spain comes to him in a flash:

> Признаюсь, меня вдруг как будто молнией осветило. (207)

His inspiration about the dog's letters had been expressed in a similar fashion:

> Сегодня однакож меня как-бы светом озарило. (200)

In both cases the idea of madness is played with. After stealing Medzhi's letters he says of the girl who lets him in:

> Я думаю, что девчонка приняла меня за сумасшедшего, потому что испугалась чрезвычайно. (201)

Similarly in his new role as King of Spain, he cannot understand how he could ever have thought of himself as a titular councillor:

> Как могла взойти мне в голову эта сумасбродная мысль. Хорошо, что еще не догадался никто посадить меня тогда в сумасшедший дом. (207–8)

The dog's letters had been a device to gain at least some form of access to the private world of the director and his daughter. Now, as the King of Spain, he needs no such intermediary. He boldly enters their apartment and

---

[18] Gustafson (op. cit. (n. 14), 273–4) interprets the dates as an attempt to avoid the unlucky number 13.

[19] Gukovsky comments that the items about the two cows is worthy of Bulgarin's paper *Severnaya pchela* (op. cit. (n. 10), 309), and that in Poprishchin himself Bulgarin recognized a reader of his paper (ibid. 305).

surprises Sofi at her toilet. His words to her are not violent, but his animosity against her seems to be expressed in his statement that woman is in love with the Devil. When he goes on to say that the Devil beckons to a woman from the star of an order worn by some stout man, and she will marry him, it is obvious that he is associating the Devil with decorations and rank, and expressing his annoyance at Sofi's preference for the gentleman of the bed-chamber (much as earlier when he had objected that it was impossible for a Donna to ascend the throne of Spain, he had again been giving expression to his mistrust of the thirst of women for rank and privilege).

As the King of Spain he no longer feels awe for the director and, deigning to visit the office, he refuses to stand up when the director enters:

> Он пробка, а не директор. Пробка обыкновенная, простая пробка, больше ничего. Вот которою закупоривают бутылки. (209)

The comparison of the director to a cork is apt—he is the apex of a closed system, and exerts pressure on all below him (his quality of 'silence' succeeds in 'bottling up' Poprishchin's emotions).[20] It also suggests medical imagery, and may be related to Poprishchin's earlier description of the face of the head of section as an apothecary's phial(198), and his later statement, which seems to reflect his disappointment over the dog's letters:

> Что письмо? Письмо вздор. Письма пишут аптекари . . . (211)

It is hardly surprising that one so in need of medical care should draw on the apothecary's shop for imagery to identify his persecutors.

His earlier lapses as a copying clerk now become marks of his greatness. When he is given a document to sign in the office he puts the signature 'Ferdinand viii' in the place reserved for the director himself. The state of his writing even leads him to some interesting discoveries:

> Я советую всем нарочно написать на бумаге Испания, то и выйдет Китай.[21] (212)

He is able to carry off his new role completely. Yet he realizes that he needs a royal cloak (for in Gogol' clothes make the man[22]) and he is reduced to cutting up his new civil service uniform to make one. He waits for the Spanish deputies to come and take him off to Spain. At last they arrive, but they are, of course, men coming to take him to the lunatic asylum. Even here the harsh reality of his situation cannot penetrate his protective delusion:

---

[20] Gukovsky relates Poprishchin's statement to the expression 'глуп как пробка' (ibid. 315).

[21] His other discovery that every cockerel has a Spain and 'that it is situated under its feathers' (*PSS*, iii, 213) could also be an oblique reference to writing (под перьями—'under feathers'/'under pens') and may perhaps be interpreted as one of his own 'экивоки и придворные штуки' as King of Spain. But perhaps most significant of all is that Испания is a jumbled version of писания ('writing'). His new-found greatness thus stems directly from the flaws inherent in his old status.

[22] The reason Poprishchin gives for not accosting Sofi when he sees her in the street is that he is wearing a dirty and outmoded overcoat (*PSS*, iii, 194) and he feels that he would be the equal of the head of section if only he had a dress-coat made by a fashionable tailor and a tie such as his head of section wears (ibid. 198).

the shaved heads of the inmates he interprets as belonging to monks at his court; the chief warder is the court chancellor; and when he is beaten and cold water poured over his shaven head, he takes these torments for the harsh customs of the land, but later is inclined to think that his court has fallen into the hands of the Inquisition. His delusion, it appears, can accommodate everything, until his very last entry, when suddenly a moment of lucidity breaks in, and in a very moving and justly celebrated passage he bemoans his fate and longs for his mother to take pity on her poor sick child. But the glimpse of reality is only momentary. The work ends with:

А знаете ли, что у французского короля шишка под самым носом? (214)

The word шишка ('lump'), suggesting a painful disorder, could be seen as a veiled reference to the abdication of Charles X after the revolution of 1830. Because of difficulties with the censor Gogol' substituted the Bey of Algiers for the King of France, but still managed to preserve a real political allusion, for in 1830 Hussein Pasha, the last Bey of Algiers, had been deposed by the French.[23]

It is true that the work has a political dimension. There are not only allusions to events abroad (in Spain, France, England, Algiers), but also criticism, which strikes nearer home—of the civil service, of the whole system of ranks and the emptiness of honours, of bribery in provincial government offices and corruption higher up (i.e. the senior civil servants (чиновные отцы) who claim to be patriots but are only interested in making money (209–10)). Of course, all these criticisms may be explained away as merely the ravings of a madman, but nevertheless it remains a fact that there is much in the story which is critical of Russian society in a fundamental way— an aspect of the story which has been emphasized by Soviet commentators.[24] In Russian cultural history the whole question of the interrelationship between 'madness' and outspoken criticism of society is one of lasting importance. Perhaps, in some measure, there lies behind it the traditional role of the 'holy fool' (*yurodivyi*).[25] Chatsky, the hero of Griboedov's *Gore ot uma*, is pronounced mad by the society he criticizes. In 1836 (the year after the appearance of *Zapiski sumasshedshego*) Chaadaev published his first *Lettre philosophique*—an outspoken attack on Russian history, culture, and society. For this he was officially pronounced mad and placed under the supervision of a doctor: he attempted to justify himself by writing *L'Apologie d'un fou*. In 1892 Chekhov restated the problem of social awareness viewed as madness in his story *Palata No. 6*, as did Gor'ky in *Foma Gordeev* (1899). The theme has become even more prominent in the twentieth century.

The present study has been an attempt to trace the fate of Poprishchin and to show that his notes are a very carefully conceived and realistic record

[23] See D. Magarshak, *Gogol: a Life* (New York, 1969), 120. Poprishchin had earlier referred to the political troubles in France: 'Эка глупый народ французы! Ну, чего хотят они? взял бы, ей-богу, их всех, да и перепорол розгами!' (*PSS*, iii, 196).

[24] See, for example, Gukovsky, op. cit. (n. 10), 313; V. V. Ermilov, *Genii Gogolya* (M., 1959), 235–7.

[25] E.g. Nikolka in Pushkin's *Boris Godunov*.

of a decline into madness. The story is unique in Gogol''s *œuvre* in that it is
the only sustained instance of the author getting inside a character. Gogol''s
methods of presenting psychology are usually 'external', that is to say people
are usually portrayed through objects and things which are associated with
them, but are nevertheless external to them (the clearest example of this is
Nevskii prospekt—which also treats the subject of madness, though in a
different context). Indeed in *Shinel'* the narrator disclaims all possibility of
getting inside another person and knowing what goes on in his mind.[26] Yet
in *Zapiski sumasshedshego* Gogol' has done just this. Poprishchin, nonetheless,
is a typical Gogolian character—like Pirogov (*Nevskii prospekt*), like Akaky
Akakievich (*Shinel'*) he is a nonentity—he is told as much by his head of
section. The strange thing is that Gogol' does not abandon his methods of
'external' presentation of psychology even here; for the only true phenomena
of Poprishchin's inner world are the random phenomena of the external
world—dogs, events in Spain, noses on the moon. All these are things with
which Poprishchin has no visible connexion—yet they come rushing in to
fill the vacuum of his inner psyche. This is how Gogol' portrays madness.
Perhaps the strangest thing of all is that it is only when the external world
can be equated with the inner world that Gogol' feels able to 'get inside' a
human being and 'know everything that is going on there'.

   Zapiski sumasshedshego has essentially the same theme as *Shinel'*: the problem
of preserving human and individual values within a framework of ranks, in
which everyone's 'content' is determined by 'form'. Both titular councillors
are obsessed by writing as the only activity which gives them status. The
perfection of Akaky Akakievich's handwriting has engulfed the whole of his
existence and made him something less than human: the imperfections of
Poprishchin's written style are symptomatic of an underlying insecurity
which ultimately drives him into madness.

   Despite the similarity of theme, the two stories, as we have seen, differ
radically in their methods. *Zapiski sumasshedshego* has been overshadowed
by the more famous *Shinel'*, but in many respects it is its superior. There is
more obvious humour, more genuine pathos, more outspoken social criticism
in *Zapiski sumasshedshego*. Moreover, it is strange that *Shinel'* should have
been acclaimed for its realism, when its substructure is bizarre to an extreme.
Zapiski sumasshedshego is in many ways the very reverse: it is a story which on
the surface is bizarre, but on closer examination proves to be thoroughly
realistic.

[26] *PSS*, iii, 159.

The Skobelev Phenomenon: the Hero and his Worship

By HANS ROGGER*

'The people need a hero, a saint—General Skobeleff, Feodor Kusmich, Ivan the Terrible—they are all alike to them. And the more remote, the more vague, the less accessible the hero, the more freedom for the imagination, the easier it is to live. There must be a "Once upon a time there lived" about it—something of the fairy tale. Not a God in heaven, but here, on our dismal earth, someone of great wisdom and monstrous power. . . . I tell you, I know the people! . . . They need the power of a great unit, of a great entity, even though that entity be zero: they will fill the zero with their own imagination, yes, yes!'

Maxim Gor'ky, relating the statement of an unrepentent monarchist made to him in May 1917. *Fragments from My Diary* (New York, 1924), 275–6.

MIKHAIL DMITRIEVICH SKOBELEV is not one of the towering figures of Russian history. He is remembered, if at all, as a general in the Russo–Turkish war of 1877–8 and as one of Russia's empire builders in Central Asia. Diplomatic historians may recall that two unauthorized anti-German and anti-Austrian speeches he made in 1882, the year of his death, caused a brief flurry of excitement and alarm in Europe's chancelleries and some annoyance to the government in St. Petersburg.

Yet in the last five years of his life, and for some time afterwards, Skobelev was the most famous and popular man in the nation. Russians and foreigners, newspapermen and diplomats, memoirists, littérateurs and even a historian or two called him the idol of the Russian people, the first man in Russia after (and sometimes before) the tsar, the Red Panslavist and people's hero, the Slavonic Garibaldi.[1] His name was known and his picture hung in the lowliest peasant hovel, brought there in the pedlar's pack along with icons, kerchiefs, and cheap prints on which our hero often appeared surrounded by mythical and historical figures of the national pantheon.[2]

He could be seen in magic lantern shows in the villages and in *tableaux*

* The author dedicates this essay to the Warden and members of St. Antony's College, Oxford, in whose pleasant and hospitable company he did much of his reading about Skobelev in the spring of 1972.

[1] For a few of many such mentions see: W. Goerlitz. 'Michael Skobelew: der rote Panslawist', in his *Russische Gestalten* (Heidelberg, 1940), 163–82; B. Nolde, *L'Alliance franco-russe* (Paris, 1936), 281; O.K. [Ol'ga Novikova], *Skobeleff and the Slavonic Cause* (1883), ch.v. For others, see nn. 2–6 below and the opening pages of G. K. Gradovsky, *M. D. Skobelev* (Spb., 1884).

[2] H. Troyat, *Tolstoy*, tr. N. Amphoux (Garden City, 1967), 199; F. Harris, *My Life and Loves* (New York, 1963), 232; A. N. Engel'gardt, *Iz derevni* (M., 1937), 202–3; Andrey Biely, *The Silver Dove*, tr. G. Reavey (New York, 1974), 43; *Russkie vedomosti*, 26 June 1882; B. Chicherin, *Vospominaniya* (M., 1934), 99; Rutkowski, 'Skobelew' (see n. 7), 148.

vivants at city fairs.[3] Streets, squares, towns, and ships were named after him;[4] music and poetry, plays and stories were composed in his honour or memory.[5] He was described as the Godfrey of Bouillon of the Slavonic race and a modern Chevalier de Bayard, as a man of Napoleonic stature with all the qualities of a people's tribune or military dictator, the equal of Suvorov, the best Russian general after Kutuzov and Ermolov, a strategist (or tactician) of genius.[6] Thirty years after his death, a monument was dedicated to him in Moscow and in January 1971 the *samizdat* journal *Veche* invoked his name with pride.

What made the victor over Turks and Turkomans the object of such veneration and the cause for such an outpouring of hyperbole? The extent and longevity of his fame suggest an importance that goes beyond the man, his generalship, his brief performance on the diplomatic stage, and the relatively narrow circle of his articulate admirers. Skobelev's importance lies less in what he said or did—in that respect his neglect by historians is entirely understandable—than in what he became: a symbol, the object of a minor cult, the heroic embodiment of certain national qualities, virtues, and yearnings. It was the hero's worship, not the hero, that appeared worthy of further study; the creation, enlargement, and perpetuation of his image that might be of value to the understanding of opinion and opinion-making, of states of mind and feeling in late Imperial Russia. Although the subject of this essay is not Skobelev but the Skobelev phenomenon—the rise to prominence and popularity of a soldier who left no lasting impact or legacy—it is necessary to relate those aspects of his life and career that became the building blocks of his legend.[7]

[3] N. Voronovich, *Vechernii zvon* (New York, 1955), 24; A. B. Naumov, *Iz utselevshikh vospominanii* (New York, 1955), i, 218.

[4] C. Marvin, *The Russian Advance towards India* (1882), 309; E. Smirnov, 'K kharakteristike M. D. Skobeleva', *Istoricheskii vestnik*, cxxxvii (1914), 957; V. A. Sukhomlinov, *Vospominaniya* (Berlin, 1924), 86; G. Shavel'sky, *Vospominaniya* (New York, 1954), 37; S. S. Fabritsky, *Iz proshlogo* (Berlin, 1926), 19; V. N. Shakhovskoy, *Sic transit gloria mundi* (Paris, 1952), 11.

[5] P. Dukmasov, *Vospominaniya o russko-turetskoi voine 1877–78 i o M. D. Skobeleve* (Spb., 1889), 435; P. L. Yudin, 'Iz rasskazov o M. D. Skobeleve', *Russkii arkhiv*, xxxix (1896), 616–18; K. K. Sluchevsky, *Sochineniya* (Spb., 1898), ii, 91–3, 165–6; Gorchakova, 'Belyi general', in A. P. Strusevich, *Bogatyr' Skobelev*, 2-e izd. (Spb., 1912), 5–6; Sh. Levin, *Kindheit im Exil* (Berlin, 1935), 295; E. Zalesova and A. Sokolova, *Belyi general. Drama* (M., 1903); Ya. Smolensky, 'Nevesta belogo generala: istoricheskaya povest'', *Kolos'ya* (1884), iii, 112–81, iv, 1–36.

[6] R. W. Kinnaird, 'The Russian Bayard: Personal Reminiscences of General Scobeleff', *The Fortnightly Review*, xxxviii (1882), 405–19; Marvin, *Russian Advance* (n. 4), 125; Novikova, *Skobeleff* (n. 1), 113; B. von Bülow, *Denkwürdigkeiten* (Berlin, 1931), iv, 564; Rutkowski, 'Skobelev' (n. 7), 95; M. M. Filippov, *M. D. Skobelev* (Spb., 1894), 78; A. A. Polovtsov, 'Dnevnik', *Krasnyi arkhiv*, lxvii (1934), 170; *Russkoe slovo*, 5 June 1911; *Russkie vedomosti*, 28 June 1882; *Moskovskie vedomosti*, 27 June 1882; N. P. Mikhnevich, *Vliyanie noveishikh tekhnicheskikh izobretenii na taktiku voiny* (Spb., 1898), excerpt in L. G. Beskrovny, ed., *Russkaya voennoteoreticheskaya mysl' XIX i nachala XX vv.* (M., 1960), 417.

[7] Basic biographical information from the entry on Skobelev by P. Geisman and A. Bogdanov in *Russkii biograficheskii slovar'*, xviii (Spb., 1904), 564–84 and N. N. Knorring, *General Mikhail Dmitrievich Skobelev* (Paris, 1939). Although the work of an admirer, Knorring's is the only serious and sober biography of the general. For the diplomatic aspects, see H. Herzfeld, 'Bismarck und die Skobelew Episode', *Historische Zeitschrift*, xlii (1930), 279–302, and E. R. von Rutkowski, 'General Skobelew, die Krise des Jahres 1882 und die Anfänge

Skobelev was born on 17 September 1843. His father was a general, as his grandfather, Ivan Nikitich, had been. The latter, beginning service as a private soldier, attained high rank (and entry into the hereditary nobility) during the Napoleonic wars—by his own sword, as the grandson would remind his men. The family's first soldier, Nikita, rose no higher than the rank of sergeant in the late eighteenth century. Skobelev and his admirers stressed his 'democratic' origins and the absence in Russia of rigid class barriers to block the recognition of merit among a richly endowed people. One of the chief architects of the Skobelev cult quotes him as telling his peasant soldiers that they too could become generals, like his peasant grandfather.[8]

While this was true—at least for their children and grandchildren—it was also exceptional. By the second half of the nineteenth century, noble lineage not only facilitated access to the upper reaches of all branches of state service; for the highest military posts it was almost indispensable.[9] This fact was appreciated by Skobelev's mother, Ol'ga Nikolaevna Poltavtseva, who brought to her husband and son, besides the estate of Spasskoe Selo, valuable connexions at court and in society. A sister married Count A. V. Adlerberg, friend and court minister of Alexander II, who was on more than one occasion his nephew's protector. Her three daughters became the wives of wealthy aristocrats. For Mikhail, the mother arranged a marriage with Princess N. Gagarina in 1874. It was dissolved after an early separation and was without issue.[10]

If it is true that Skobelev was as friendly with the poorest as with the most powerful and wealthy, it is among the latter that he moved, their style of life that he followed, their values that he absorbed and their help that he enlisted. The wine and champagne he liked to drink, the fine linen, perfumes, and splendid white uniforms he wore, were more characteristic of his tastes than the soldier's soup, which he, like Suvorov, occasionally ate out of the common kettle with his men. His defiance of social and military conventions was itself an aristocratic trait.[11]

---

der militärischen Vereinbarungen zwischen Oesterreich–Ungarn und Deutschland', *Ostdeutsche Wissenschaft*, x/xi (1963/4), 81–151, which is invaluable for the reports of Austrian military and diplomatic agents in Russia.

[8] 'Rodoslovnaya Skobelevykh', *Russkaya starina*, xii (1878), 527–8; Filippov, *Skobelev* (n. 6), 5; Kinnaird, 'Russian Bayard' (n. 6), 406; I. A. Chantsev, *Skobelev kak polkovodets* (Spb., 1883), 136; S. F. von Ditmar, 'Pamyati M. D. Skobeleva', *Mirnyi trud*, 1907 no. 6, pp. 163–4; Novikova, *Skobeleff* (n. 1), 3, 133; B. L. Mozdalevsky, *ed.*, 'Skobelevy, ded i vnuk', *Russkaya starina*, xcv (1898), 61–4.

[9] It is true that Generals M. V. Alekseev, the son of a poor soldier, and A. I. Denikin, the grandson of a serf, attained high rank and important positions, and that by 1895 only about half of all officers were hereditary nobles. But the noble officers continued to predominate in the guards and to hold most important commands. Of the army's 130 full generals, 97.5 per cent were of the hereditary nobility at the turn of the century; among 410 lieutenant-generals it was 96 per cent. See P. A. Zaionchkovsky, *Samoderzhavie i russkaya armiya na rubezhe XIX–XX stoletii, 1881–1903* (M., 1973), 202–14.

[10] 'Rodoslovnaya Skobelevykh' (n. 8), 528; Filippov, *Skobelev* (n. 6), 1, n. 5.

[11] D. A. Milyutin, *Dnevnik* (M., 1947–50), iv, 143; V. V. Vereshchagin, *Na voine v Azii i Evrope* (M., 1894), 207; F. V. Greene, *Sketches of Army Life in Russia* (New York, 1880), 140.

The boy was taught at home until the age of twelve by a German tutor whose severity he resisted and resented. The conflict between the German pedant and the headstrong, high-spirited Russian child was later seen as a clash of national temperaments which shaped and foretold Skobelev's feelings about Germany and the Germans, as did his devotion to D. Girardet, the owner of a boarding school in Paris where the boy was placed after the German's dismissal. The Frenchman's less rigorous methods were so successful and the boy's attachment to him so great that Ol'ga Nikolaevna induced him to move to Russia with his charge. There, Mikhail was prepared for the university and enrolled in the mathematics faculty at St. Petersburg in 1860. It is not known who or what determined that choice, nor why an unruly and not very studious youth, who was envious of other young men who already had their officer's epaulets, should have entered the university at all.[12]

Fortunately for him, student disorders closed the university in the autumn of 1861 and shortly afterwards Skobelev was accepted by the aristocratic regiment of Horse Guards as a cadet private. At last he wore the uniform on which he vowed to pin his grandfather's St. George's Cross which he considered his inheritance and carried in the lining of his coat. He became a senior cadet (*portupei-yunker*) in 1862, was promoted to cornet in 1863 and to lieutenant in 1864.

There was little to set Skobelev apart from other young guardsmen, unless it was the crude extravagance of his pranks and amusements. Only after he had tasted combat and glory and become possessed by that intoxicating mixture did his comrades and superiors take notice of him, his vanity, his vast ambition, and the restless energy which served it. Never a comfortable friend or willing subordinate—a lonely childhood had not prepared him for friendship or team-work—and fully at ease only with those of inferior rank or abilities, he was able to wrest even from those who disliked him a measure of admiration for the very strength of his determination to win fame and popularity. His comrades made fun of his need to be liked, of the lengths to which he would go to woo those who resisted him, but they also took seriously the hero's pose he assumed. 'How he managed it', one of them wrote much later, 'I still do not know, but I do know that there was not then any reason for it.'[13]

He went to Warsaw in February 1864 as aide to Adjutant-General E. T. Baranov, but soon transferred to the Grodno Hussars who were then in action against the remnants of the Polish insurrection. Although Polish resistance was nearly over, there were still engagements with fugitive guerrillas and for his bravery in one of these Skobelev was awarded the order of St. Anne (fourth class). The insurgence quelled, he took leave to observe the war between Prussia and Denmark, but it had ended by the time he reached the theatre of operations. For two years he wandered with remarkable freedom

[12] V. I. Nemirovich-Danchenko, *Skobelev: lichnye vospominaniya i vpechatleniya*, 3-e izd. (Spb., 1903), ii, 82; Filippov, *Skobelev* (n. 6), 62; Mozdalevsky, 'Skobelevy' (n. 8), 65–7; *Russ. biogr. slovar'*, xviii, 565; Knorring, *Skobelev* (n. 7), 14–15.

[13] Baron N. Vrangel', *Vospominaniya* (Berlin, 1924), 134.

and frequency from one place or assignment to another until he was admitted to the General Staff Academy in 1866.[14]

A more logical choice than the university, it was hardly a happier one. During his second year he no longer attended lectures, neglected his work and was generally regarded as a loafer and playboy who would never amount to much. He did not even seem to take much joy in his extra-curricular escapades. One of his teachers described him as an unsmiling, grey-faced, moody young man who lacked all the attributes of youth—vigour, beauty, freshness and charm. On the point of resigning from the Academy, he was persuaded that it was the only way of realizing his soldierly ambitions. On graduation he was placed twelfth among twenty-five classmates who were given staff appointments.

It was his command of languages, his wide if eclectic reading, his knowledge of strategy and history, and possibly his social standing and connexions that allowed Skobelev to make as good a showing as he did. According to some, it was his unorthodox solution of a field exercise.[15] Ordered to find a suitable place to cross a river, he drank vodka in a local tavern instead of reconnoitring the terrain, and when the examining committee arrived, threw himself into the stream at the nearest point, swimming his mount across and back without mishap. This incident too was said to foreshadow later ones, both in its daring and theatricality. It could also be taken as a sign of recklessness when Skobelev recommended it in 1877 as a method for moving a large body of cavalry across the Danube under fire. Promoted in 1868 to *shtabs-rotmistr*, he was attached to the staff of General K. P. von Kauffmann, conqueror and Governor-General of Turkestan, where he arrived early in 1869.

Central Asia was Russia's India and Algeria, the place where it was possible to build an empire and one's fortune, the testing and training ground for officers bored by peace-time garrison duty and frustrated by the slow climb up the ladder of ranks. There, M. G. Chernyaev, the 'Lion of Tashkent', had made a name for himself, and there hundreds of others hoped to do likewise. But neither staff work nor the command of a *sotnya* of Cossacks on raids along the Bokharan frontier offered enough scope for Skobelev's energy, which found an outlet in dissipation. Quarrels with fellow officers who felt that he had stretched the limits of truth in reporting on his actions led to duels and a public reprimand from Kauffmann, followed by assignments in Russia and the Caucasus before Skobelev was allowed to return to Central Asia.[16]

At the Ministry of War, he became the subject of an inquiry by Dmitry Milyutin. In a letter of 30 September 1870, Kauffmann described his

[14] On Skobelev's years in Poland and at the General Staff Academy, see A. Vitmer, 'Chto videl, slyshal, kogo znal', *Russkaya starina*, cxxxiv (1908), 609–708.
[15] There are different versions of this story, involving different rivers and motives, including a wager.
[16] Vereshchagin, *Na voine* (n. 11), 325–6. D. Mackenzie's *The Lion of Tashkent: the Career of General M. G. Cherniaev* (Athens, Georgia, 1974) suggests some striking similarities in the characters and careers of the two men, as well as differences which help to account for Skobelev's greater and more lasting popularity.

troublesome subordinate as a capable officer whose energy and enthusiasm were not, however, matched by thoroughness and application. He would do well with troops in the field, but was not cut out for administrative duty of which he would quickly tire. 'His excessive ambition, his desire to outshine and outdo others, cause him to be indifferent as to the means employed. He lost my confidence through an untruth of which he even boasted. His comrades detest him, and there is one episode after another in which he is the guilty party.' Kauffmann denied the rumour of Skobelev's cowardice which had caused him to fight two duels and would have led to more if he had not been stopped.[17]

On the outbreak of the Franco–Prussian War Skobelev asked, and was denied, permission to fight with the Prussians. Instead, he was posted to the Caucasus, where he spent less than a year, leaving under a cloud. It appears that he exceeded his orders while on reconnaissance in the region of Krasnovodsk and prematurely revealed Russian intentions towards the Khanate of Khiva.[18] Although this did not block his advancement—he became a lieutenant-colonel in 1872—the taint of scandal which attached to him had become permanent. When the general advance on Khiva was begun early in 1873, Skobelev managed to join it. On 28 May, with most of the Russian force at the walls of Khiva, Kauffmann negotiated its surrender. Entry was to be effected the next day without firing on the city or its inhabitants. Skobelev disobeyed this order, and while he may, in this instance, have followed the instructions of his immediate superior, Kauffmann was displeased with him. The belief persisted that he wished to garner cheap laurels by fighting enemies who had already yielded—although some may, in fact, have continued to resist. There was even a rumour, stubborn enough to be repeated fifty years later, that Skobelev, 'who was something of a sadist', had amused himself, while drunk, by chopping off the heads of prisoners.[19]

Khiva did much to fix his reputation for needless display and cruelty; it also validated his claim to his grandfather's inheritance. To determine why one of the Russian columns had failed to link up with the rest and what disposition to make for its further movement, it was necessary to explore the territory it had still to traverse—a forbidding desert full of hostile tribesmen. After some hesitation on Kauffmann's part, Skobelev was given the task he had asked for and discharged it with skill and courage. The feat won him the coveted St. George (fourth class), although approval by other members of the order was neither unanimous nor prompt; it also brought him to the attention of Russia and the world and laid the basis for the Skobelev legend.

In its making no small part was played by J. A. MacGahan (then of the *New York Herald*), one of Skobelev's journalistic friends and admirers during

[17] Milyutin, loc. cit. (n. 11).

[18] M. D. Skobelev, 'Zapiska o zanyatii Khivy, 1871', *Ist. vestnik*, x (1882), 130–8; F. A. Wellesley, *With the Russians in War and Peace* (1905), 19–20.

[19] E. Tolbukhov, 'Skobelev v Turkestane, 1869–1877', *Ist. vestnik*, cxlvi (1916), 112–19; E. Schuyler, *Turkestan*, 4 ed. (1876), ii, 349; V. I. Gurko, *Features and Figures of the Past* (Stanford, 1939), 446.

the Turkish war. The two men first met 'on the banks of the Oxus, in the Khanate of Khiva', just after the 'remarkable and daring expedition'. MacGahan helped to give currency to the story of that exploit in which a brilliant Russian officer, disguised in native dress, accompanied by two Russian and three native horsemen (in other versions he had only one or two Khivan companions), outwitted nature and scores of wily enemies. More important, he observed and described with care the area he had reconnoitred, demonstrated that he could be cautious and deliberate as well as impetuous, and regained the good opinion of Kauffmann, who became his steadfast advocate and defender.[20]

On his return to Russia in late 1873, Skobelev was received by the Tsar, promoted to colonel, and given the signal honour for one so young and notorious of being named aide-de-camp (*fligel'-adyutant*) to the sovereign and appointed to his suite. Despite all these signs of favour—perhaps because of them—the military establishment remained cool to him, as it was to many officers who had made their reputations in colonial campaigns where performance was not measured by the conventional standards of warfare against more formidable enemies than the native 'night-gowns' were believed to be. When Skobelev, after observing the Carlist War on the rebel side, asked to command a squadron of dragoons in Tbilisi, he was turned down and posted to the *guberniya* of Perm' to help administer the new conscription law. By May 1875 he had made his way back to Kauffmann and Tashkent to take an active and prominent part in the conquest of Kokand. The khanate was incorporated into the Empire as the Ferghana region (February 1876) and Skobelev was appointed its military governor.

He was now, at thirty-two, a major-general, holder of a second St. George (third class), the order of St. Vladimir (third class), and other awards. He had shown, as a cavalry commander in the Kokand campaign, that he could lead units larger than raiding or reconnaissance parties—even Milyutin was pleased with him—and he discharged his administrative duties at Ferghana to the entire satisfaction of Kauffmann. Yet, he was still taxed with insubordination, recklessness and cruelty. There were complaints that he had needlessly risked the lives of the 150 Cossacks with whom he had attacked an enemy camp of six or seven thousand at night; that he had rushed to be the first to enter Kokand without concerting his movements with those of other detachments; that he had engaged in acts of terror against non-combatants; and finally, that he was guilty of abusing his gubernatorial powers.[21]

Envy helped to launch these accusations: envy of such a quick rise on the part of a man who played so little by the rules; envy of the protection he enjoyed from his relatives and from Kauffmann. Skobelev's masterful character and lack of modesty created resentment, as did his strictures against

[20] Vereshchagin, *Na voine* (n. 11), 328–9; Tolbukhov, 'Skobelev' (n. 19), 660; J. A. MacGahan, *Campaigning on the Oxus and the Fall of Khiva* (New York, 1874), 427–8, and idem, *Deistviya na Oksuse i padenie Khivy* (M., 1875). For MacGahan's later recollections of the meeting, see *The War Correspondence of the 'Daily News'* (1878), i, 82. Cf. Goerlitz, 'Skobelew' (n. 1), 166.

[21] Nemirovich–Danchenko, *Skobelev* (n. 12), ii, 129–39; Milyutin, *Dnevnik* (n. 11), i, 224; Smirnov, op. cit. (n. 4), 957–8; Tolbukhov, 'Skobelev' (n. 19), 370–402.

the personal enrichment which many colonial administrators considered their due. There were veiled hints also of personal misconduct, of 'family troubles'. It is impossible to say with certainty what happened during Skobelev's year-long governorship of Ferghana and why he left it. Was it at his own request, to defend himself against charges of malfeasance or peculation? Was he removed? Or did he simply, with or without permission, go to St. Petersburg to ask to join the Army of the Danube for the war with Turkey?[22]

Alexander, who had been told of Skobelev's 'reprehensible behaviour', received the hero of Kokand in spite of it. It was a strange audience. The Tsar would not shake hands with him, praised him for his bravery, and said that he could not do so 'for the rest'. Then, with some agitation and in a raised voice, he added: 'I knew and remember your grandfather and blush for his illustrious name'. A confused Skobelev was dismissed with the admonition to prove himself in his next assignment. A chilly meeting with Milyutin, who adverted to irregularities in Ferghana, did not reassure him, nor was he given a command. An aide of Kauffmann's gave the most concrete indication of the sources of displeasure.

The points of the indictment against him are: looseness of discipline and conduct among the troops; excessive familiarity with the officers; democratization; and a deliberate policy of discriminating against the bearers of great names. . . . The Minister of War supplemented his comments by saying that the Tsar had been unfavourably impressed by letters he had received from Kokand that Skobelev had been too intimate with his officers, that members of the staff had too freely criticized the government, and that he had contemplated organizing a march on Kashgar.[23]

Skobelev had indeed drawn up plans for an expansion of Russia's territory in the direction of Kashgar (whose emir had displaced the Chinese) and for a possible incursion into India, a 'demonstration' which was to weaken England's support of Turkey and make her more amenable to Russian wishes in the Eastern question. They were no more than 'feasibility studies' and may have been invited or tacitly encouraged by Kauffmann. And if he loosened the rigidities of military etiquette on a colonial frontier or showed his contempt for the well-born and well-connected who sought a quick taste of fire and easy fame, all of it hardly accounts for Alexander's blushing for him or the general reticence about his misdeeds. Skobelev could be irreverent, he was genuinely concerned about the welfare of his subordinates and receptive to their views, but he was no subverter of discipline, neither a social nor a political rebel, and certainly no democrat. The belief that he was something

[22] Ibid. 657–60; R. Furneaux, *The Siege of Plevna* (1958), 25; Chantsev, *Skobelev* (n. 8), 165; A. A. Sigov, 'Dragomirov i Skobelev', *Ist. vestnik*, cxxiv (1911), 183; and Skobelev's letter to Kauffmann of 2 June 1877 in *Ruskii arkhiv*, xlviii (1910), 623.
[23] Letter of Gen. V. N. Trotsky, 12 March 1877, in Tolbukhov, 'Skobelev' (n. 19), 663; D. D. Obolensky, 'Nabroski iz proshlogo. Graf E. I. Totleben i M. D. Skobelev', *Ist. vestnik*, lix (1895), 96–100; idem, 'Eshche o Skobeleve i Totlebene', ibid. 902; Milyutin, *Dnevnik* (n. 11), iv, 144; Knorring, *Skobelev*, (n. 7), 69–73.

of a *frondeur* arose because of the events of later years and because several of his detractors were titled courtiers.[24]

Skobelev's eclipse in the early stages of the Turkish war, which began on 12 April 1877, only served to make his star shine more brightly when other generals failed to win the quick victories they had been expected to achieve. This could not, of course, have been predicted, least of all by Skobelev himself, who was alternately in despair and rage over the indignity of being passed over for any kind of responsible task. He was attached to the headquarters of the Grand Duke Nikolay for 'disposition', that is, he was free to seek employment where he could find it, mostly as a 'volunteer' in minor skirmishes, for a time as acting chief-of-staff in his father's Cossack division. In mid June he took part in the crossing of the Danube under M. I. Dragomirov, who generously acknowledged Skobelev's help. His calmness under fire, the effect this had on those who had never seen combat, his willingness to act as Dragomirov's orderly officer—a position usually filled by captains or lieutenants—were rewarded by a medal and marked the beginning of his rehabilitation.

It was the lack-lustre performance of others as much as the young major-general's own successes that won the reluctant admission of his claims. The prejudice persisted that he was little more than a dashing *sabreur*, as did the belief that for the sake of personal glory he would fail to come to the aid of colleagues and would sacrifice his men. Yet Russian reverses before the Turkish stronghold of Plevna and Gurko's retreat over the Balkans made it difficult any longer to deny Skobelev's skilful management of ill-assorted and hastily assembled units, his ability to inspire them by his courage and concern for their well-being. In September, after a third assault on Plevna had been beaten back with such great losses that the Grand Duke advocated withdrawing behind the Danube, Skobelev came into his own. Promoted to lieutenant-general, he was given command of the 16th Infantry Division which had lost half its officers and men and which he quickly rebuilt into an effective force.[25]

The symbol of boldness in the eyes of the public, Skobelev remained for most senior commanders the personification of rashness and self-advancement. When the hero of Sevastopol', E. I. Totleben, was entrusted with the conduct of operations in the field and firmly held to a blockade of the Turkish garrison at Plevna, the stage was set for a clash of personalities and policies that went beyond the issue of the moment. The clash was muted at first by differences in rank and responsibilities and by a measure of mutual respect. Totleben called Skobelev 'a hero such as one rarely finds, *mais un homme sans foi, ni loi*'. Skobelev, in turn, valued the other's Crimean experience, his theoretical knowledge and engineering skill. But when the investment of Plevna lasted for weeks and months, he could not contain his impatience.

[24] 'Proekt M. D. Skobeleva o pokhode v Indiyu', *Ist. vestnik*, xiv (1883), 543–5; 'Posmertnye bumagi M. D. Skobeleva: Pis'ma s Kashgarskoi granitsy, 1876 g.', ibid. x (1882), 109–38 and 'Turkestan i angliiskaya Indiya', ibid. 275–94; V. T. Lebedev, *V Indiyu* (Spb., 1898), 10; Schuyler, *Turkestan* (n. 19), ii, 280; Marvin, *Russian Advance* (n. 4), 160–1.

[25] Vereshchagin, *Na voine* (n. 11), 108–9, 332–7; *Russ. biogr. slovar'*, xviii, 573–6; M. A. Gazenkampf, *Moi dnevnik, 1877–1878 gg.* (Spb., 1908), 41, 67.

He took aggressive actions to provoke both Turks and Russians into engagements which would force the latter on to the offensive and a renewed assault
on Plevna. Totleben repeatedly restrained the younger man's ardour and on
one occasion threatened him with a court-martial.[26]

Disagreements over timing and tactics were exacerbated by Skobelev's
eagerness to make them public. The conflict became one of youth and age,
Russian spirit and German method, fervent patriotism and cautious calculation. To the officers, journalists and visitors who came to his hospitable
camp and table, the commander of the 16th Division freely criticized the
temporizing of his superiors, the passivity to which the 'German general'
condemned a force superior to that of the enemy. Why waste time and
strength on a prolonged siege when winter would make it more difficult to
cross the Balkans and achieve a swift victory before the European powers
could come to Turkey's aid? 'At only one point of the line is there anything
like enterprise', wrote an English newspaperman, 'and that is where General
Skobelev is.'[27]

The White General (as the newspapers called him because of the colour
of his dress and charger) and the Panslavists with whom he was now identified, were right in their suspicions that Totleben had little enthusiasm for the
war. 'We became involved in it because of the fantasies of the Panslavists and
the intrigues of the English.' The sacred cause of liberating fellow Christians
and fellow Slavs left him cold. He was convinced that the Bulgarian peasants,
who were better off than their liberators, wished to be rid of them as soon as
possible.[28] It was over the objections of Totleben, who favoured a gradual
wearing down of the enemy, that the Grand Duke, after the capitulation of
Plevna (28 November), won the Tsar's approval for pursuit of the Turks and
a rapid advance on Constantinople. It was for his part in that last stage of the
campaign—the hard-fought passage through Shipka pass, the battle of
Sheinovo—that Skobelev was celebrated in prose, in poetry, and on canvas,[29]
as well as criticized again for having 'intentionally delayed' coming to the
aid of other units 'on mean grounds of personal interest . . . to appear the
hero of the battle'.[30]

Other generals might still regard him 'as an officer with whom, in time of

[26] Ibid. 173; V. I. Nemirovich-Danchenko, *God voiny*, 2 ed. (Spb., 1879), i, 263; D. I.
Ilovaisky, 'Poezdka pod Plevnu v 1877 g.', *Russkaya starina*, xxxvii (1883), 351–74; 'Zapiski
P. M. Gudim-Levkovicha o voine 1877–1878 gg.', ibid. cxxiv (1905), 566–71; V. Herbert,
The Defence of Plevna (1910), 311–12; Filippov, *Skobelev* (n. 6), 41–4.
[27] *War Correspondence . . . 'Daily News'* (n. 20), ii, 4.
[28] Filippov, *Skobelev* (n. 6), 43–4.
[29] V. V. Vereshchagin's painting 'Skobelev at Sheinovo' was exhibited in Moscow in
January 1880 and widely reproduced. See A. A. Vereshchagin, *U bolgar i zagranitsei*, 2 ed.
(Spb., 1896), 149.
[30] R. von Pfeil, *Experiences of a Prussian Officer in Russian Service* (1898), 209. The debate
whether Skobelev had or had not withheld assistance to other units continued for decades. See
V. Frank [H. von Samson Himmelstjerna], *Russland, seine Hilfs- und Machtmittel* (Paderborn,
1888), 22; V. Dmitrovsky, 'Radetsky i Skobelev v srazhenii 27-ogo i 28-ogo dekabrya 1877
pod Shipkoi', *Russkaya starina*, cvi (1901), 594–624; S. A. Dragomirova, 'Skobelev', *Ist.
vestnik*, cxxxix (1915), 796–803; A. Vitmer, 'Eshche o M. D. Skobeleve', ibid. cxl (1915)
901–7; A. Wolkoff-Mouromtzoff, *Memoirs* (1928), 171–2; Furneaux, *Siege* (n. 22), 89.

peace, no one would shake hands',[31] but he was now a popular idol and received important assignments and marks of imperial favour. He led the advance guard to the outskirts of Constantinople, commanded the army of occupation in western Turkey, and organized a militia in Eastern Rumelia. In the summer of 1878 he was placed at the head of 4th Army Corps at Adrianople and appointed Adjutant-General. His rehabilitation appeared to be complete, despite the fact that he shared the view of Ivan Aksakov and many others (not all of them Panslavists) that Russian policy had been indecisive about war aims and that the gains of San Stefano should not have been surrendered at the Congress of Berlin.[32]

He was said to have asked the Grand Duke Nikolay to let him only take Constantinople—he could afterwards disavow him and have him shot. The victory won in the field, Skobelev complained, was but half a victory; if the troops were not to occupy Tsargrad, they should at least have had the satisfaction of marching through the city and dictating peace there, however generous its terms. Even without the conquest of the Bosphorus, greater concessions could have been exacted from Turkey and the threat of English intervention checked by activating his plan for an invasion of India, raising rebellion there and the spectre of social revolution in the English homeland.[33]

Skobelev did not seek to mobilize support for his position except through private letters and conversations. Perhaps, like the government, he realized the risks of renewed war; perhaps he did not wish to endanger his standing with the Tsar. He had reason to take care that popular acclaim did not become a liability. As early as October 1877, Senator A. A. Polovtsov had noted that the general's renown grew by the day and that when he passed their tents, the soldiers would rush out to shout 'hurrah'—'which they usually did only for the Tsar'.[34] The royal receptions given the returning warrior in several cities in April 1879 gave rise to apprehension at court, and in order to avoid giving offence, Skobelev cancelled visits to Moscow and other towns. An assignment to observe the German manoeuvres (from which he returned convinced of German hostility) and the training of his 4th Corps at Minsk for a time kept him out of the limelight.[35]

Discretion was rewarded by his appointment to lead the expedition sent in 1880 against the Turkomans of Akhal–Tekke. Their raids had frustrated efforts to pacify Transcaspia; the expedition of 1879, under General N. P. Lomakin, had ended in ignominious defeat. The spectacle of a mighty power unable to prevail over 20,000 primitive tribesmen was deeply disturbing to the Tsar and his advisers, especially after their retreat before the European

[31] von Pfeil, *Experiences* (n. 30), 209. Gazenkampf, an aide to the Grand Duke Nikolay, called Skobelev a 'national hero', a 'demi-god to his men', and his loss, if he should die of a wound he had received, 'an all-Russian misfortune' (*Moi dnevnik* (n. 25), 173, 180).

[32] V. P. Meshchersky, *Moi vospominaniya* (Spb., 1898), ii, 381–2.

[33] N. I. Nemirovich-Danchenko, *Na kladbishchakh. Vospominaniya* (Revel', 1921), 86; idem, *Skobelev* (n. 12), ii, 79–80; Filippov, *Skobelev* (n. 6), 61; Lebedev, *V Indiyu* (n. 24), 10; 'Zapiska general-adyutanta M. D. Skobeleva 27-ogo dekabrya 1878 g., Adrianopol'', *Russkaya starina*, xxxv (1882), 227–32.

[34] A. A. Polovtsov, 'Dnevnik', *Krasnyi arkhiv*, xxxiii (1929), 176; von Pfeil, *Experiences* (n. 30), 208.

[35] Knorring, *Skobelev* (n. 7), 149–54.

powers. The prestige of Russian arms had to be restored, and the choice of Skobelev was logical and sound, given his experience in Central Asia and his well-known championship of national honour and greatness. He was for the first time commander-in-chief of an enterprise which he himself planned from its very beginning and saw through to a successful conclusion—the capture, on 12 January 1881, of the Tekke stronghold of Geok-Tepe and the utter defeat—some called it a massacre—of the survivors.[36]

As had been true in the Balkans, Skobelev's achievements were enhanced by prior failures and by his carefully composed dispatches. The enemy he faced was not his equal and the rejoicing over the victory, therefore, out of proportion to its magnitude and significance. Nevertheless, there were formidable problems of climate and communications; in dealing with them Skobelev showed as never before his administrative and organizational talents.[37] Even doubters, remarked Milyutin (and he was one of them), had now to admit that Skobelev had perseverance as well as energy: 'The brilliant success at Geok-Tepe . . . has undoubtedly restored our position not only in Transcaspia but in all of Asia.'[38] The Tsar was pleased— Skobelev was promoted to full general and decorated with another St. George (second class)—and national sentiment was gratified.[39] Dostoevsky in his journal exulted over the triumph of Russian arms and the impression it would make on Asia's millions: 'Long live the Geok-Tepe victory! Long live Skobelev and his good soldiers!'[40]

After the tension of battle, the object of all this praise suffered a depression. He was physically exhausted and emotionally drained, restless and irritable, not willing to immerse himself in the routine of colonial administration. He must have wished to garner the fruits of his fame at first hand rather than hear of them at a distance. He asked to be replaced, pleading illness, but he was still in Transcaspia when a bomb killed Alexander II on 1 March 1881. The news deepened his depression; the new tsar had stricter standards of conduct than his father and disliked Skobelev as much as he was disliked by him.[41]

Skobelev's ambitions—they were widely agreed to be vast, if vague—were unlikely to be realized in the new reign. His expectations of an outpouring of popular adulation and of the Tsar's antipathy were both fulfilled on his

[36] Marvin, *Russian Advance* (n. 4), 258; Rutkowski, 'Skobelew' (n. 7), 89. Cf. A. W. Wereschtagin, *Skobelew im Türkenkriege und vor Achal-Teke*, tr. A. von Drygalski (Berlin, 1907), 168–9.

[37] V. Shakhovskoy, 'Ekspeditsiya protiv Akhal-Tekintsev . . .', *Russkaya starina*, xlvi (1885), 161–84, 377–410, 531–58; A. F. Artsishevsky, 'M. D. Skobelev v ego pis'makh i rasporyazheniyakh vo vremya Akhal-Tekinskoi ekspeditsii, 1880–1881 gg.: ocherk i ego sobstvennoruchnye rasporyazheniya', ibid. xxxviii (1883), 387–432; Marvin, *Russian Advance* (n.4), 190; idem, *The Eye-witnesses' Account of the Disastrous Russian Campaign* (1880), 135.

[38] Milyutin, *Dnevnik* (n. 11), iv, 17.

[39] H. L. von Schweinitz, *Denkwürdigkeiten* (Berlin, 1927), ii, 142; *Russ. biogr. slovar'*, xviii, 578–81.

[40] *The Diary of a Writer*, tr. B. Brasol (New York, 1954), 1044. For Ivan Aksakov's comments in *Rus'*, see *Sochineniya*, vii (M., 1887), 275–85.

[41] O. F. Geifel'der [Heyfelder], 'V Zakaspiiskoi oblasti, 1879–1887. Vospominaniya vracha o M. D. Skobeleve', *Russkaya starina*, lxxv (1893), 181–216; Wereschtagin, *Skobelev* (n. 36), 183.

home-coming in April. The very fervour of the crowds who met the victor of
Geok-Tepe on his way to the capital was viewed with envy or alarm by a
ruler who was fearful of showing himself in public, shunned ceremonial
functions, and had withdrawn to the fortress-like Gatchina Palace. In Moscow a crowd of 25,000, many more than the police expected, met Skobelev's
train, tried to unhitch the horses of his carriage and to carry him on their
shoulders. The Governor-General of the city barely made his way to the
platform to greet the hero and was obviously shaken by the experience:
'*J'ai vu hier Bonaparte revenant d'Egypte*'.[42] Spontaneous street demonstrations,
even patriotic ones, were frightening to officialdom. Foreign diplomats had
predicted as much, even before Skobelev set foot on Russian soil.

They had been reading the country's mood, and especially that of the
upper classes in whose midst they moved and whose opinions they recorded.
Fear that the nihilist conspiracy was still a danger to the monarch and the
dynasty was deepened by the isolation of the régime. Its abandonment of the
so-called Loris-Melikov Constitution, which Alexander II had approved
shortly before his assassination, the dismissal of three of his ministers, and
the reaffirmation of autocracy in the manifesto of 29 April 1881 distressed
many conservatives as much as liberals. The threat of revolution, they
believed, could not be met by police methods alone or by the reassertion of
imperial and bureaucratic prerogatives. Some way had to be found, short of
representative institutions, to allow men of property and prominence a share
in the business of government, to give it a broader basis of support and to
make it more responsive to the nation's needs.

No one realized better than the chief author of the new course, Konstantin
Pobedonostsev, how much it had alienated the literate public. In this
predicament he impressed upon the Tsar the necessity of attaching to himself
a man who could be of great value in time of need. Having learned that
Skobelev would reach St. Petersburg in a matter of days, Pobedonostsev
wrote on 4 May:

> I know your Majesty did not like him. I am not acquainted with him per-
> sonally, but it seems to me that he was much maligned before you. At the
> same time, he is a power in the army and among the populace and, by all
> reports, a very able and inspiring man. I believe that his devoted assistance
> and service may become necessary to your Majesty on many occasions, and
> it is therefore most important how he will be received. I take the liberty of
> saying: let him leave you with satisfaction, not with a cold feeling but with
> fervent loyalty to you.[43]

Alexander could not overcome his antipathy, and Skobelev's version of the
audience became the talk of the salons. The Tsar had granted him a bare ten
minutes, had not invited him to sit down, and had shown little interest in the
Akhal–Tekke expedition beyond voicing displeasure at the death of the young
Count Orlov in the fighting and inquiring what the state of discipline among
the troops had been.[44]

---

[42] Obolensky, op. cit. (n. 23), 107; Ditmar, op. cit. (n. 8), 156.
[43] *Pis'ma Pobedonostseva k Aleksandru III* (M., 1925–6), i, 338.
[44] Vrangel', *Vospominaniya* (n. 13), 135–6; E.-M. de Vogüé, *Journal* (Paris, 1932), 286.

Pobedonostsev was sufficiently alarmed by what was being said 'in town' to write another letter in which he chided his former pupil for disregarding good advice and the precariousness of his throne. One should not deceive oneself, he lectured; these were stormy times requiring great prudence, with the greatest dangers still ahead. There was the unhappy possibility that Russia would divide for and against the Tsar. At such a critical time he had to win to his side the nation's best, those who could not only speak but also act and of whom, alas, there were all too few.

Perhaps, as they say, Skobelev is a man without conscience. So be it! But remember, your Majesty, that there are not many great captains in history one could call virtuous, and yet they moved and decided events. It is possible for a man to be immoral in his personal life and yet be the carrier of great moral forces and to have vast moral influence over the masses. Skobelev, I say again, has become such a force and has gained great influence over the masses, that is to say, people believe in him and follow him. That is terribly important, now more than ever. . . .[45]

Pobedonostsev, a congenital worrier and pessimist, exaggerated the peril of the monarchy, but he assessed correctly the effect Alexander's frigidity would have on the temperamental general. A more generous acknowledge-ment of his worth might have made him more tractable; in the event, he was driven into opposition and forced to formulate his discontents more clearly and to voice them more openly than he had ever done before or probably wished to do. Denied influence and prominence at court or in the army, he sought both in the country. For a Russian general it was an unprecedented step, a measure of the injury his pride must have sustained. To return to the 4th Corps at Minsk, to provincial boredom and anonymity, appeared impossible for the moment and Skobelev took leave abroad.

His bitterness and political actions stemmed not from wounded vanity alone. He had, after all, criticized the timidity of Russian foreign policy long before the accession of Alexander III and the unfortunate interview. Still, that event was a turning-point and disabused him of any hopes he may have built on the fact that the new tsar more nearly shared his views on the Straits, the Balkans, and the Germans than did his father.

Although for Skobelev politics meant exclusively the question of Russia's strength and standing among the powers, the new reign and the debates over what course it should follow increased his awareness of public affairs. He could not but take a greater interest in domestic matters—they were being discussed in every drawing-room—and see a connexion between the state's conduct at home and abroad. He was neither a liberal nor, in culture or domestic politics, a Slavophile. His position on the political spectrum is difficult to fix and it is unknown where he stood on the issues which agitated everyone in 1881: a constitution, a Muscovite assembly of estates, or Western representative institutions. He was certain, however, that reaction was not the answer to nihilism and that the reforms of Alexander II which had helped to make serfs into citizen soldiers and patriots had to be preserved.

[45] *K. P. Pobedonostsev i ego korrespondenty* (M., 1923), 232–5.

'There were fanatical Panslavists who wanted to go back into the night of time, but he was not one of them.'[46]

It is the imprecision and the sparsity of Skobelev's ideas that made him appear more threatening than he was. During his European trip, for example, in the early summer of 1881, he not only saw Gambetta, with whom he was linked in a common hatred of Germany, but also met Loris-Melikov and supposedly offered himself as the fallen minister's arm for carrying out indefinite plans against the Tsar. Loris declined, and afterwards observed that there was no guarantee that a month or two later the fiery general would not propose similar action of which he, Loris, would be the target. It is hard to see how the man who was regarded as the tool or (with more justice) the ally of Ignat'ev and Aksakov, the embodiment of their anti-liberal chauvinism, could even approach the author of the Loris-Melikov constitution, the *bête noire* of Slavophiles and reactionaries.[47]

An unpopular administration, which was still uncertain of its hold on power, could not dismiss lightly the rhetoric of a popular general. The government felt so beleaguered on all sides that it kept secret the renewal of its alliance with Germany and Austria (6 July 1881), the very powers that had helped to rob Russia and her allies of the full fruits of victory. Improved relations with the Germanic states could not, however, fail to become known; they were opposed not only by the nationalist press (especially by Aksakov's *Rus'* and less vehemently by Katkov's *Moskovskie vedomosti* and Suvorin's *Novoe vremya*), but also by the Minister of the Interior and author of the Treaty of San Stefano, N. P. Ignat'ev, who was thought to be Skobelev's protector.[48] In a conversation with Count P. A. Valuev in July, Skobelev told the Chairman of the Committee of Ministers (as he had told others) that war with Germany was inevitable and was the only way of solving Russia's economic and political crisis, 'even the dynastic question'.[49] At about the same time he said to friends that the autocracy would be swept

[46] Marvin, *Russian Advance* (n. 4), 311; see also p. 125: 'What he would do in the event of a revolution in Russia time alone can tell, but his role would not be an insignificant one.' Aksakov said much the same: 'There is no doubt that Skobelev will have a great role to play in Russian history. . . . It is difficult to say whether this role will be good or bad, but it will be great in any case.' (Quoted in S. Lukashevich, *Ivan Aksakov* (Cambridge, Mass., 1965), 160.) Nemirovich-Danchenko wrote that the general had imparted to him his domestic political programme, which he was not at liberty to reveal. In spite of its promising title, D. D. Kashkarov's *Vzglyady na politiku, voinu, voennoe delo i voennykh M. D. Skobeleva* (Spb., 1893) contains only one chapter related to political matters, and that deals exclusively with foreign affairs. An unsigned article in *Russkoe slovo*, 'Skobelev v pis'makh', of 5 June 1911, concluded that although Skobelev was a Slavophile, he did not so much believe in the necessity of a *zemskii sobor* as in the establishment of a legal order, and that for all the intensity of his nationalism he was opposed to the repression of the Empire's non-Russian nationalities. Also see Knorring, *Skobelev* (n. 7), 196–204, for the general's positive appraisal of the reforms of Alexander II, especially as these affected the army.

[47] Ibid. 191; A. F. Koni, *Na zhiznennom puti* (Revel'–Berlin, n.d.), iii, 20–2; P. A. Valuev, *Dnevnik, 1877–1884* (Petrograd, 1919), 176–83; Goerlitz, *Skobelew* (n. 1), 94; letter of Konstantin Kavelin in M. K. Lemke, *ed.*, *M. M. Stasyulevich i ego sovremenniki v ikh perepiske* (Spb., 1912), ii, 158.

[48] I. Grüning, *Die russische öffentliche Meinung und ihre Stellung zu den Grossmächten* (Berlin, 1929), 79; Nolde, op. cit. (n. 1), 280–1.

[49] Valuev, *Dnevnik* (n. 47), 170.

away by a revolution and that the army was not obliged under all circumstances to defend it. 'Dynasties change or disappear, but nations are immortal.'[50]

Pobedonostsev was not alone in taking such talk and the man who uttered it seriously. Foreign diplomats and military men did so and included in their dispatches news and gossip about Skobelev's words and movements. This was true not only of Germans and Austrians, who had most to fear from him; E. M. de Vogüé, secretary of the French Embassy, believed that he was preparing to play the role of a Russian Bonaparte, mentioned his 'dynastic pretensions', and called him a 'Slav Garibaldi' and 'dangerous madman'. His behaviour in late 1881 and early 1882 did indeed make him an annoyance and a potential danger to a government which felt compelled to pacify nationalist protest against a meeting of the Russian and German emperors (September 1881) by describing it as a purely family affair.

In October the Austrian military attaché informed Vienna that Skobelev was using his frequent visits to the capital—where he would come from Minsk to sit on an army reform commission—to arrange meetings with young officers of the line, whom he lectured on military and historical topics. There is no exact record of what he said, which is in any case less important than the fact of the meetings themselves and the absence from them of guards and general staff officers. Skobelev was deliberately by-passing the military élite, which he knew to be suspicious of his professional unorthodoxies, his character, and his political ideas, to address that part of the officer corps which was closest to the nation and its soldiers. This was more than an educational enterprise and less than the preparation of a coup or conspiracy. It was an effort on the general's part to gain the attention, the influence and the following the Tsar had denied him. The effort may not have been fully conscious or aimed at a clear goal, but like the constant attention which Skobelev received from the press, it served to make him a troubling presence.

One topic at these gatherings was the violence with which, beginning in November–December, the Slav population of Bosnia–Hercegovina and southern Dalmatia met Austrian imposition of conscription. For all opponents of the Treaty of Berlin (which had turned Bosnia–Hercegovina over to Austrian occupation) and of the 1881 alliance with Germany and Austria (which granted the latter the right to annex these provinces at an opportune time), this was final proof of the spineless abandonment by Russian diplomacy of Russian and Slav interests. There were renewed calls for revising the Berlin agreement and the German orientation of Russian policy. Skobelev was reported to have told his listeners that he would resign from the army to rush to the aid of oppressed fellow Slavs anywhere and that anyone who was not a coward would do likewise.[51]

In a letter of 19 November he also made explicit the connexion between the country's domestic troubles and foreign indignities at which he had hinted

[50] Vrangel', *Vospominaniya* (n. 13), 137–8.
[51] Rutkowski, 'Skobelew' (n. 7), 93–102, 148; Herzfeld, 'Bismarck' (n. 7), 279–80; de Vogüé, *Journal* (n. 44) 187, 256, 286, 294; E. Toutain, *Alexandre III et la République française* (Paris, 1929), 23; Ivan Aksakov, *Slavyanskii vopros* (M., 1886), 336; Nolde, op. cit. (n. 1), 280.

earlier. The country's non-Russian, non-national cosmopolitans, in and out of uniform, bore as much guilt for its defeats at the conference table as did Bismarck or the British fleet. The criminal surrender of Russian rights and honour before Tsargrad might still have to be paid for on the Vistula and had, moreover, contributed to the moral decline at home. 'One thing I firmly believe and proclaim: the shameful sedition which now disgraces Russia is largely the result of despair and disappointment over the peace treaty which was forced on Russia and which neither the country nor its banners deserved.'[52]

The letter had been elicited by Skobelev's reading an article by Aksakov on the Congress of Berlin, and it was to the Aksakovs and Moscow—the home of Slavophilism and Panslavism—that he went at the beginning of the new year, not to the Balkans. On 9 January the intellectual leader of Russian nationalism and its most famous exponent in action met, apparently for the first time. He explained why he had come. Times were serious, and he wanted advice and help. He had sworn fidelity to the new tsar in the hope and belief that he would usher in a national policy and end subservience to Germany. 'Instead, we find ourselves once more on that same slippery road and about to sacrifice Russia and her interests in Slavonic lands to Prussia and Austria.' When Aksakova demurred, saying that she had known the Tsar since childhood and that his patriotism was exceptionally firm, Skobelev pointed to the strength of German influence in the very bosom of the imperial family: two Grand Duchesses, with great influence over their husbands, intrigued on Germany's behalf, and one of them was an agent of Bismarck.

When Skobelev told him what he planned to say at a banquet commemorating the fall of Geok-Tepe, Aksakov cautioned moderation, showing himself to be a better judge of public opinion than readers of his fiery editorials would have believed. He persuaded the general not to call for a public subscription on behalf of the anti-Austrian insurgents; coming from a prominent officer it would be tantamount to a call for war and the government would be forced to disavow him. Moreover, such a subscription had no chance of success. The country was afraid of war and would overome its apathy and indifference only if it were attacked. The initiative for a break had to come from the outside. The Aksakovs learned also of Skobelev's meetings with Gambetta and suspected that the arrival in St. Petersburg of Juliette Adam, Gambetta's friend and revanchist editor of the *Nouvelle Revue*, was part of an effort—in which they thought Ignat'ev and Katkov might be involved—to bring about a Franco–Russian understanding and an anti-German alliance.

The Aksakovs wondered whether the Tsar had tacitly sanctioned this effort or whether he was its target. Their visitor's main purpose, they felt, had been to learn from them the state of public opinion on the question of war, but they did not think that he had fully revealed himself or his intentions. 'It is all rather hazy', Aksakova observed, 'but in the midst of the present chaotic situation, where everyone is vague and indefinite, a strong will and a burning ambition, such as are combined in Skobelev, could

---

[52] From F. I. Bulgakov, 'Pamyati M. D. Skobeleva', *Ist. vestnik*, ix (1882), 399–400; for similar remarks made to Valuev, see his *Dnevnik* (n. 47), 187–8.

easily seize the reins and turn Russia in what direction they will.' To some
that prospect seemed less remote after the Geok-Tepe anniversary speech of
12 January 1882 before an audience composed mostly of officers. When
Valuev heard of it, he called the speech impossible; the man who had made
it reminded him of a Spanish general with a '*pronunciamento* in his pocket'.
The German ambassador told the Foreign Minister Giers that Skobelev
was more dangerous to the Russian government than to foreign ones.[53]

What he had said was not, in fact, terribly novel or inflammatory,
although an active general giving a political speech to active officers at a
public dinner was unprecedented in a country where political speeches were
rare. In an unmistakable reference to Bismarck's 'blood and iron', Skobelev
had implied that German might should not and would not always make
right; he had taken to task the intelligentsia, Russia's home-grown cosmopolitans, for separating themselves from the larger Slav family as well as
from their own people, and for being the last to respond when tsar and
nation called; finally, he had spoken words of sympathy for those who were
defending the Orthodox faith and Slavonic nationality on the shores of the
Adriatic against German–Magyar rifles and militant Austrian clericalism;
he had concluded by affirming his belief in Russia's historical destiny and
mission.[54]

The Tsar might be in sympathy with these sentiments, but he could
hardly endorse rebellion against a brother-monarch and ally. And Skobelev
made it more difficult for the authorities to ignore him by his belligerent talk
in officers' messes and salons. It was as if he were disappointed that his speech
had not had a greater resonance. To one hostess he expressed the wish that
steps would be taken against him; he would then resign from the army and
go to the Balkans with money and guns. 'To overthrow the Prince of Bulgaria?' he was asked. 'No, I shall make him powerful, if he will join me'—
presumably in the unification of his country and in the violation of existing
treaties and agreements. When at last the Tsar expressed his displeasure and
a trip abroad was suggested to Skobelev, he went to Paris in late January
1882.[55]

His welcome there was predictably warm. He met with Juliette Adam and
Gambetta and delivered himself of some forceful opinions which found their
way into the press. The effect was all he could have wished for and only a
little less dramatic than his appearance in Eastern Rumelia would have
been. The speech which Skobelev gave on 5/17 February to a group of
Serbian students who had called on him justified the fears of the cautious
directors of Russian policy, gave pause even to the more enterprising among

[53] The Aksakov–Skobelev meeting is described in A. F. Tyutcheva, *Pri dvore dvukh impera-
torov. Dnevnik, 1855–1882* (M., 1929), 230–3; see also Valuev, *Dnevnik* (n. 47), 181; Schweinitz,
Denkwürdigkeiten (n. 39), ii, 182.
[54] K. Arsen'ev, *Za chetvert' veka* (Petrograd, 1915), 110–22; Rutkowski, 'Skobelew' (n. 7),
100–1; Novikova, *Skobeleff* (n. 1), 259–61; Aksakov, op. cit. (n. 51), 390, 413–24, 433.
[55] Schweinitz, *Denkwürdigkeiten* (n. 39), ii, 183; Nemirovich-Danchenko, *Skobelev* (n. 12), ii,
141. According to Filippov (*Skobelev* (n. 6), 71, 87), the general had openly talked of his hopes
of occupying the Bulgarian throne, and then of an invitation, extended by Prince Alexander,
to become Bulgarian minister of war, with a promise from the Prince to provoke a quarrel
with the Turks within two years. Although he was tempted, Skobelev refused the post.

them (i.e. Ignat'ev),[56] and caused so great an uproar in foreign offices and embassies as to make inevitable the general's recall and some form of chastisement.

He had told the Serbian students why Russia did not always live up to her patriotic obligations and Slav mission: it was because in internal as well as external affairs she was under an alien influence. Russians were not masters in their own house; the foreigner had penetrated everywhere; his hand was in everything. 'He dupes us, makes us the victim of his intrigues, the slaves of his power. . . . We are so subjugated and paralysed by his pervasive and ruinous power that if we are . . . to free ourselves . . . we shall be able to do so only by force of arms.'

Skobelev then named the alien intruder, the intriguing usurper, the enemy of Russia and all Slavs—'it is the author of the *Drang nach Osten* . . . it is Germany'.

I repeat it, and ask you never to forget it—Germany is the enemy. A struggle between Slavs and Teutons is inevitable, but I believe that it will culminate in the victory of the Slavs. As for you, it is natural that you should yearn to know how to act, since the blood of your people is already being shed. I shall not say much, but I can assure you that if anyone ventures to touch the states recognized by European treaties, whether it be Serbia or Montenegro . . . you shall not be left to fight alone. . . . If fate wills it, we may meet again on the field of battle, shoulder to shoulder against the common enemy.[57]

His government was persuaded to recall Skobelev by German and Austrian protests, and by the still more compelling arguments of its ambassador to France, who observed that the general was openly playing the role of a Garibaldi. 'It is necessary to take strong action in order to demonstrate that a general cannot make such speeches outside of Russia with impunity and that only the Tsar has the right to decide questions of war and peace.' In view of what Kaiser Wilhelm had reputedly said on learning of the speech— 'My nephew no longer has an army!'[58]—it was essential to prove him wrong.

However, what the Kaiser regarded as insubordination went unpunished. Despite an official disclaimer of the Paris remarks as private and unofficial, despite assurances that Alexander had severely reprimanded his general, the latter, it quickly became known, emerged from an audience of two hours with every sign of satisfaction and happiness. He even boasted of having set out for the Tsar his idea that only war could save the dynasty, that only after victory would he be able to return to his capital and live there in safety. What a contrast with the earlier meeting of the two men at which Skobelev had not been allowed to raise questions of policy! General P. S. Vannovsky, the Minister of War, reflected the sovereign's change of attitude: 'The Tsar loves Skobelev and sympathizes with his true Russian sentiments.' He was neither dismissed nor demoted, and the revision of the service regulations

---

[56] *Pobedonostsev i ego korrespondenty* (n. 45), 83.

[57] 'Rech' generala Skobeleva v Parizhe v 1882 g.', *Krasnyi arkhiv*, xxvii (1928), 215–25; Novikova, *Skobeleff* (n. 1), 254, 276; Marvin, *Russian Advance* (n. 4), 306–8.

[58] 'Rech' . . . Skobeleva' (n. 57), 218; E. A. Perets, *Dnevnik* (M.-L., 1927), 125.

forbidding political speeches by military men was sufficiently general not to appear an affront to one individual.[59]

Calculation as much as love or sympathy lay behind the decision not to discipline the errant soldier. Ignat'ev may have pleaded his case; the Tsar may have heeded Pobedonostsev's warning; he still had much backing in the country and in the army, perhaps more than before the Paris speech. On his arrival from Warsaw—where he had stopped to toast the Poles as brother-Slavs and to warn them of the German danger—he was met by several hundred people, most of them young, many of them officers. Servants and small tradesmen were said to be his enthusiastic admirers and to predict that he would suffer for his attacks on the Germans. Several regiments offered him testimonial dinners or requested his picture; both they and Skobelev were given to understand that this was inappropriate and should be stopped. In the cities in which elements of his 4th Corps were stationed, populace and clergy turned out to offer the traditional bread and salt. 'Russia is more taken with this man today than with the invisible Tsar of Gatchina', Vogüé noted.[60]

If that was the reason for his gingerly treatment, it also made it advisable not to appoint him to a post of greater prominence or power than he held. Vannovsky, conceding that he would make an excellent commander-in-chief, also thought it risky to entrust him with a corps on the western frontier, where he might provoke clashes with Germans and Austrians. For the time being, it would be safest to post him to Turkestan.[61]

Skobelev died on 26 June 1882, before a decision had been made about his future. In the last months of his life he was despondent and moody. Far from contemplating new undertakings, he seems to have realized that he had been put on the shelf and that the moment for greatness had passed him by. With the dismissal of the mercurial Ignat'ev in May and the appointment of Dmitry Tolstoy, a no-nonsense administrator, as his successor, the government again felt firm ground under its feet and saw less need to heed the public clamour. The diplomatic storm had subsided; the domestic crisis was about to be contained.

Skobelev's sudden death at the age of 39 made it certain that his image would remain bright, that he would be remembered as a dauntless young warrior of uncompromising patriotism and great promise who would have done still greater things for the fatherland if a cruel fate had not struck him down before his time. In a way, his death was the highest achievement of his life, for it brought him all the recognition and respect, praise and piety he could have wished. There are few figures in Russian history who were celebrated and mourned as he was at his death.

[59] Ibid. 127; G. A. de Vollan, 'Ocherki proshlogo', *Golos minuvshego*, 1914 no. 6, p. 135; Schweinitz, *Denkwürdigkeiten* (n. 39), ii, 190; Nolde, op. cit. (n. 1), 282; Herzfeld, 'Bismarck' (n. 7), 296; Milyutin, *Dnevnik* (n. 11), iv, 168; *Pobedonostsev i ego korrespondenty* (n. 45), 386, n. 62; Rutkowski, 'Skobelew' (n. 7), 121–3, 133.

[60] Vogüé, *Journal* (n. 44), 294; Marvin, *Russian Advance* (n. 4), 283: 'He is more than ever the idol of the army and the people'; R. von Pfeil, *Neun Jahre in russischen Diensten unter Alexander II* (Leipzig, 1907), 32; Knorring, *Skobelev* (n. 7), 251–2.

[61] Perets, *Dnevnik* (n. 58), 127.

Estimates of the size of the crowds who paid their last respects to him in Moscow vary, but there is no disagreement that they were huge and, as noted by many observers, composed for the most part of people of the lower classes. During the period of mourning the newspapers carried reports of peasants and merchants, provincial dignitaries and military men attending memorial services in villages and cities.[62] They also told of official plans to issue a volume of Skobelev's letters and miscellaneous writings for distribution to the troops,[63] and of the resolution adopted by the St. Petersburg duma to build a monument in that city.[64] In the latter half of 1882 there also began the production of a considerable Skobelev literature—biographies, reminiscences, pamphlets, articles, fiction—which by 1902 was sufficiently large to warrant the publication of a bibliography.[65]

It is doubtful whether all this would have come to Skobelev in such rich measure if he had not died when he did. As a Viennese newspaper put it: 'Skobelev had been forgotten, but now he is remembered again'.[66] If he had lived to an old age, perhaps in provincial obscurity or self-imposed foreign exile, he might have disappeared from public view, as did Chernyaev and other military heroes of his generation. He felt and feared this himself, and a fellow officer who saw him shortly before his death predicted that Skobelev would choose suicide over an obscure old age.[67] He might, conceivably, have overcome his dejection if he had been called to be commander-in-chief or minister of war. That, however, was most unlikely. Neither Alexander III nor his son, Nicholas II, would have wished to see this unpredictable and masterful man in positions of such power and prominence where, even if he had no thought of removing the monarch, he could easily overshadow him.

If the hero's early death made possible the continuing worship of him, his exaltation was greatly assisted by sinister interpretations of the circumstances in which he died. It was never doubted or denied that he suffered a fatal heart attack in a brothel. Although this was carefully kept out of the newspapers, it was widely known and not necessarily considered damaging by his devotees and comrades. 'His end was wonderful', one of them said.[68] While Russian tolerance for the weakness of sinful man is proverbial, and Skobelev's was an all too human death, it lacked dignity and grandeur, the stuff of which legends are made. It was, Aksakova thought, an inglorious end. It

---

[62] V. V. Yasherov, 'Kak umer Skobelev', *Russkii vestnik*, 1904 no. 10, pp. 740–50; Tyutcheva, op. cit. (n. 53), 234; Nemirovich-Danchenko, *Skobelev* (n. 12), ii, 119–27; M. I. Polyansky, *Pamyati M. D. Skobeleva* (Spb., 1908), 86–90; Ditmar, op. cit. (n. 8), 167–8; Tolbukhov, 'Skobelev' (n. 19), 107; Novikova, *Skobeleff* (n. 1), 387–92; Chantsev, *Skobelev* (n. 8), 142–53.

[63] Only his orders were actually collected and published: *Prikazy generala M. D. Skobeleva*, ed. A. N. Maslov (Spb., 1882).

[64] Aksakov protested that St. Petersburg had no right to the monument, which should be erected in Moscow. It was, but not until 1912.

[65] M. I. Polyansky, *Bibliograficheskii ukazatel' literatury, otnosyashcheisya k biografii M. D. Skobeleva* (Spb., 1902). I was unable to locate a copy of this work. The most recent addition to the literature of the Skobelev cult of which I am aware is G. Mesnyaev's *Polya nevedomoi zemli* (Munich, 1962), 7–122.

[66] *Wiener Allgemeine Zeitung*, 15 July 1882.

[67] 'Zapiski N. G. Zalesova', *Russkaya starina*, cxxxiv (1905), 6.

[68] Harris, op. cit. (n. 2), 232.

was made to seem less sordid, more noble, more tragic and meaningful by a spate of stories and rumours that he had been killed and that the one or more ladies with whom he had spent his last night had been the instruments of his demise.[69]

Suspicions that he had met foul play were ascribed to the *vox populi*, to the cabmen, porters, letter-carriers and *meshchane* whose sound sense and patriotic instincts supposedly made them question the official announcement: since he had died shortly after supper and had many enemies and rivals, he must have been poisoned. Another source of suggestions that Russia's favourite had fallen victim to a plot was the anti-German press of France. In a booklet on Skobelev first published in 1886, Juliette Adam hinted broadly that she knew the true cause of his death. On the evening preceding it he had called on Ivan Aksakov and had spoken of his impending doom. 'And who', Adam asked, 'could have had an interest in removing the hero whose motto has been: "The German, there is the enemy"?' Later editions of her booklet carried a footnote to the Paris speech saying that Skobelev had paid for it with his life. 'Bismarck had him assassinated.'[70]

For those who gave credence to the charge there was further proof in the nationality of Skobelev's companions during the fatal night. They were German, and Wanda, the one most often mentioned, became known as 'Skobelev's Tomb'. From the *Intransigeant* of Henri de Rochefort came the allegation that it was his own countrymen who wanted him out of the way and had drugged and strangled the man who was more dangerous than any nihilist because the entire army would follow him against the government. Prince Peter Kropotkin, in his memoirs, repeated the tale, which he attributed to Loris-Melikov, that when Alexander III ascended the throne and 'hesitated to convoke the Assembly of Notables', Skobelev proposed to Loris and Ignat'ev that he arrest the Tsar and compel him to sign a constitutional manifesto. Ignat'ev allegedly denounced the scheme to the Tsar.[71]

In 1917, just after the fall of Nicholas, there appeared in a respected journal a communication which was the first published elaboration in Russia of gossip which had long circulated there. The author reported what he had heard from Sergey Muromtsev, the Kadet President of the first Duma. Having become convinced that Skobelev was plotting to overthrow the Romanovs, the government set up a secret tribunal of forty persons to try the general *in absentia*. Thirty-three of its members voted for the sentence of death and charged a police official with carrying it out. Police agents accomplished the deed in the establishment in which Skobelev was being enter-

[69] Tyutcheva, op. cit. (n. 53), 234; Valuev, *Dnevnik* (n. 47), 201. In an article of 1 January 1883 Aksakov spoke of Skobelev and Gambetta as having died under mysterious circumstances (*Sochineniya* (n. 40), vii, 678–88). Cf. Yasherov, op. cit. (n. 62), 745–7; Bülow, *Denkwürdigkeiten* (n. 6), iv, 564; Vollan, op. cit. (n. 59), 143; Tolbukhov, 'Skobelev' (n. 19), 107–8; W. A. Apuschkin [V. A. Apushkin], *Skobelew über die Deutschen* (Berlin, 1922; first published in St. Petersburg in 1914 as *Skobelev o nemtsakh: ego zavety slavyanstvu*), 6.

[70] J. Adam, *Le Général Skobeleff*, 5 ed. (Paris, 1916), 57, n. 1; 63.

[71] Yu. Kartsov, *Sem' let na Blizhnem Vostoke, 1879–1886* (Spb., 1906), 95; N. P. Meshchersky, letter of 10 March 1887 in *Pobedonostsev i ego korrespondenty* (n. 45), 727; O. Novikova, *Russian Memories* (New York, 1916), 86; P.U., 'Zagranichnaya pechat' o Rossii v 1882 g.', *Ist. vestnik*, xi (1883), 198; P. Kropotkin, *Memoirs of a Revolutionist* (New York, 1962), 278.

tained. Pretending to be young Moscow merchants out on a spree, they sent to his room a gift of poisoned champagne.[72]

Elements of this version appeared in the reminiscences which Skobelev's friend, the writer V. I. Nemirovich-Danchenko, published in 1921. He accepted the hypothesis of a secret trial and judgement but did not implicate the Tsar himself, except in the concealment of the crime. For all his faults, 'Ananas III' would not stoop to murder. The verdict had been signed by one of the Grand Dukes (most probably Vladimir, whom Skobelev once called the prince-consort of Bismarck's concubine) and Count Peter Shuvalov, former head of the Third Section and one of Russia's representatives at the Congress of Berlin. It was they and the hired assassins of the Holy League (the secret counter-revolutionary organization) who had considered the future Suvorov too great a danger to the autocracy to allow him to live.[73]

None of these theories was ever substantiated. They contain obvious improbabilities—such as a 'secret' court of forty members—and are inconsistent with one another. It was never explained, for example, why the Holy League (which, according to Kropotkin, Skobelev had been invited to join) should have been determined to destroy him almost six months after he had made his peace with the Tsar and kept it. Quite possibly he had before then, in his impetuous and blustering way, vented his annoyance with the stodgy, stubborn ruler who reduced the army's budget and refused to recognize Skobelev's greatness or follow his lead in foreign affairs. But there is not a shred of proof that Skobelev contemplated, much less prepared, the overthrow of the Tsar, of autocracy, or of the monarchy.

Even if he had favoured the purely decorative assembly of estates (*zemskii sobor*) that was the brainchild of Ignat'ev and Aksakov or backed the consultative organs proposed by Loris-Melikov, their rejection by Alexander III would not have enraged Skobelev to the point of treason. Both projects aimed at strengthening the monarchy and left unlimited the tsar's power; it would have been folly for one who advocated either to endanger or reduce that power. Skobelev did not admire or like Alexander III; he may not have cared much for Alexander II; and he definitely had little use for the court and courtiers. Yet he never lost sight of the sovereign's central position in the Russian system, of his importance as the final arbiter of policy and preferment.

Skobelev was interested in both, and, as his letters show, he was concerned not to give offence and to put in the right light actions which might be misinterpreted. Milyutin thought that his public pronouncements were not so much directed against the Tsar as pleas for his approval.[74] It is possible that he was seeking support for an active foreign policy (and incidentally for himself) from a ruler he believed to be in sympathy with his own goals and whom he was addressing over the heads of flabby bureaucrats and diplomats. 'On the bureaucratic horizon of St. Petersburg', he told Aksakov, 'the Tsar

[72] F. Dyubyuk, 'Smert' Skobeleva', *Golos minuvshego*, 1917 no. 5/6, p. 102.
[73] Nemirovich-Danchenko, *Na kladbishchakh* (n. 33), 62–8.
[74] Milyutin, *Dnevnik* (n. 11), iv, 144.

represents the only hope for a national policy at home and abroad—the Tsar and Ignat'ev.'[75] The practice of seeking the monarch's ear, of telling him truths which his advisers kept from him, was sanctioned by conservative tradition and theory. And Skobelev was a conservative monarchist in every fibre of his being, not least when he occasionally railed against the Tsar.

The persistence of the belief among adherents of the Skobelev cult that he had been the target of an aristocratic conspiracy was a measure of conservative frustration with the last two occupants of the throne. Alexander III and Nicholas II did not provide dynamic leadership for the cause of monarchy and nationalism; they were incapable of embodying the monarchical principle with heroism and intelligence; they were not popular, and they fearfully rejected men who were and who might restore the vitality of the system and its appeal.

Disenchantment with the monarch and with his unresponsiveness to society's needs and wishes had set in during the reign of Alexander II. In some this feeling was induced by his flagging devotion to reform; in others by his indecisiveness in dealing with sedition or by his reluctance to embrace the cause of liberating the Slavs. Discontent reached a high point during the dark moments of the Turkish war and in its disappointing aftermath. As respect and devotion for the Tsar declined among his subjects, Skobelev gained their regard. He was what they wished their tsars and all their leaders to be in time of war; he was an extension of themselves as they wished to see themselves. He redeemed incompetence at the top, the shame of defeats in the field and the scorn of the world. For a few short years he became Russia's emblem, her representative figure, one of the few—perhaps the only one besides the common soldier—to emerge intact and splendid from an enterprise which had raised and dashed so many high hopes.

The height of these hopes was itself the consequence of an earlier dejection of spirit and loss of vitality in government and society. Men of the most diverse outlook commented on the phenomenon and looked to Russia's involvement in the Balkans to end stagnation at home and to make good the humiliation of the Crimean War. A. S. Suvorin, publisher of *Novoe vremya*, wrote in February 1876 of 'the boredom, the melancholy mood that so many people feel; the apathy that makes people shrug their shoulders . . . tells us that they are waiting for something'. For the militant nationalist Suvorin there was no doubt what that something was and he both reflected and heightened the keen sympathy with which his readers followed events in south-eastern Europe by extensive coverage in his paper.[76]

At the opposite end of the political spectrum, the young revolutionary Lev Deich recalled the spring of 1876 as one of the most colourless moments of Alexander's reign. The period of reforms had ended and was now more than ten years in the past. Everywhere a sense of dissatisfaction, of frustrated

[75] Nemirovich-Danchenko, *Skobelev* (n. 12), ii, 141, and Apuschkin, *Skobelew* (n. 69), 46. Cf. Schweinitz, *Denkwürdigkeiten* (n. 39), ii, 191.

[76] Effie Ambler, *Russian Journalism and Politics: The Career of A. S. Suvorin* (Detroit, 1972), 108, 113, 134. Cf. P. N. Milyukov, *Vospominaniya* (New York, 1955), i, 67, and Arsen'ev, op. cit. (n. 54), 217–18.

hopes; there was little interest in internal affairs. Only what was happening in the Balkans stirred Russians out of their somnolence. Radicals too, he observed, were caught up in the general awakening; among them too there were volunteers who went to fight in Serbia and advocates of Russian intervention.[77]

Radicals were optimistic that the political interests and popular enthusiasm engendered by the fight for liberty abroad would fuel the movement for liberty at home; liberals and moderates were confident that the Tsar would recognize and reward the nation's sacrifices. The beginning of hostilities was anticipated as the beginning of a new and brighter era. Police reports show that the idea of war with Turkey was welcomed among all strata of the population. The general air of hopeful expectancy reached even the Jewish *shtetl* of Belorussia.[78] In the working-class districts of the capital a declaration of war was impatiently awaited for the 19 February, the anniversary of Emancipation. Had not an earlier war put an end to serfdom and ushered in great reforms? A more advanced, more mature people, a people more conscious of its rights, expected to have these confirmed and expanded.

The jubilation which greeted the declaration of war confirmed its popularity, as did the cheers and flowers given the departing troops. The heroine of Nemirovich-Danchenko's novel *Plevna and Shipka* may not have been typical of all Russians—it is a safe guess that few peasant or working-class families were happy to send their men to war—but her feelings were widely shared and reported, more widely than in any other conflict in which Russia had engaged. Bored and disgusted with her life, she, like the rest of the country, rejoiced at the coming of war in which she soon took part as a nursing sister, a war which bore the promise of future happiness.

Everyone who had not yet abandoned hope, everyone who had not yet lost faith in the people expected that after their baptism by fire and sword the people would begin a new life as full-fledged citizens. The war opened up new horizons; there the soldiers fought for their country's happiness. On the bloody battle-fields there was not only life, but meaning; there a new era was beginning, there a new sun was rising.[79]

First reports from the fronts in Asia and Europe, telling only of successes and advances, sustained belief in the blessings victory would bring, the more so since it appeared to be near and not too costly. The flags of celebration were almost never taken down; the Te Deums followed one another in quick succession; the war fever displaced all other concerns and grievances. Then, beginning in July, the tide of battle turned and with it the public's mood, its confidence in its leaders and in the future. Intoxication gave way to sobriety and then to sullenness or anger as Plevna was attacked twice with insufficient forces and more reserves had to be called up, as Gurko withdrew across the Balkans and the siege of Kars had to be lifted. Frightful losses and the mobilizing of the guards brought home the reality and the seriousness of the

[77] L. Deich, *Za polveka*, 3 ed. (M.–L., 1926), 262–3.
[78] Levin, *Kindheit* (n. 5), 293.
[79] *Plevna i Shipka* (Spb., 1881), pt. i, 21.

reverses suffered. 'Our military promenade', Ol'ga Novikova wrote, 'has transformed itself into a burial procession.'[80]

In salons, embassies, and clubs harsh judgements were passed on every aspect of the war's conduct, from faulty strategy to corruption in the commissary department, from a frivolous underestimation of the enemy to lack of unified operational direction. The chiefs of the armies in Asia and on the Danube, the Grand Dukes Mikhail and Nikolay, were now discovered to be unequal to their tasks, to lack military training and talent. The latter, it was said, had never been distinguished for anything but his debts and his amorous conquests. Criticism of members of the imperial family who held military commands at various levels—practically all its adult males— became particularly severe when Nikolay Nikolaevich tried on 30 August to take Plevna for his brother's name-day present at a cost of 30,000 lives.[81]

This 'name-day pie with human stuffing', as it was called in a poem of the day,[82] expressed the disillusionment which pervaded army and people and from which the Tsar was no longer immune. The feeling grew that the ruling family was more concerned with their own honour and prestige than with their subjects' lives, that monarchy and nation were no longer fighting in a common cause. Pobedonostsev, in letters to the future Alexander III who was with the army in Bulgaria, reported the complaints he heard (and shared) about Grand Duke Nikolay and his aides, their ignorance, conceit and rigidity: it was essential that a new commander-in-chief be appointed quickly. It was not done, and Pobedonostsev described the mood in St. Petersburg as nasty and ominous. 'You cannot imagine', he wrote on 3 October, 'how much everyone here, from the lowliest to the greatest, discusses and judges men and affairs. There is not a doorman, house-porter or cabman who is not ready to express an opinion, to condemn and to argue. Among this class of people there is much more agitation than there is at the top.'[83]

At the bottom, anger was turned more often (or at least more audibly) against the generals than against the Tsar or his grand-ducal relatives. The Menshevik A.N. Potresov remembered in his old age the beginning of a ditty which was making the rounds when, as a child, he first heard the name of the younger Skobelev and scorned his contemptible and luckless colleagues:

> *Shil'der, Shul'dner, Shakhovskoy—*
> *Duraki, duraki,*
> *Vse nochnye kolpaki.*
> *A nash Skobelev vtoroi. . . .*[84]

[80] Quoted in R. F. Byrnes, *Pobedonostsev* (Bloomington–London, 1968), 128.

[81] Pfeil, *Experiences* (n. 30), 4, 51; Wellesley, op. cit. (n. 18), 161–4; Valuev, *Dnevnik* (n. 47), 15; Schweinitz, *Denkwürdigkeiten* (n. 39), i, 432–8; Anon., *Russland vor und nach dem Kriege* (Leipzig, 1879), 343–5; P. K. Fortunatov, *Voina 1877–78 gg. i osvobozhdenie Bolgarii* (M., 1950), 52–3; Gazenkampf, *Moi dnevnik* (n. 25), 160, 185; F. V. Greene, *Army Life in Russia* (New York, 1885), 149–50.

[82] I. I. Popov, *Minuvshee i perezhitoe* (L., 1938), 31; Valuev, *Dnevnik* (n. 47), 117–18.

[83] *Pis'ma Pobedonostseva . . .* (n. 43), i, 69–73, 81.

[84] *A. N. Potresov, 1869–1934* (Paris, 1937), 109.

Schilder–Schuldner (like Krüdener, Shakhovskoy, Shnitnikov, Zotov, and others) was considered to be a poor general by experts as well as by the man in the street.[85] But for the latter he had the added disadvantage of a difficult foreign name which made him doubly suspect. Deciphering his name in a dispatch which reported that Schilder-Schuldner's division had been beaten back at Plevna, a tipsy factory worker told his comrades that this '*eneral*' must be a Jew.[86] Two generals with Polish names, Nepokoichitsky and Levitsky— Nikolay's chief-of-staff and assistant chief-of-staff—were rumoured, together with pro-Polish Russians, to be conspiring at nothing less than the destruction of the army. More sober opinion thought them incompetent. Popular judgements and rumours were crude reflections of what more sophisticated people were saying and writing. After the second battle of Plevna, for example, the historian D. I. Ilovaisky ended an article which was a scathing critique of the generalship displayed there with a prayer that the Lord send better leaders for Russia's valiant army.[87]

Against this background, Skobelev's glamorous, youthful figure—the average age of corps commanders at the front was 59[88]—stood out in sharp contrast, although it was not he but an old general with a German name who led the army out of its humiliating impasse and made possible the capture of Plevna. 'Plevna had fallen at last, chiefly thanks to Totleben. But when we talked of Plevna in Russia, somehow or other the name of Skobelev was always on the tongue.'[89] He was by no means the only general who emerged with his reputation intact or enhanced from a campaign which, even after its victorious conclusion, most military commentators considered to have been poorly led and planned. Yet even among those few commanders whose strategy (in the words of an English observer) had not been proved to be beneath contempt or who had not grown rich at the expense of the soldiers, Skobelev was the one most often singled out for public praise.[90]

He may not have been as good a general as he and his partisans thought; he was certainly a better one than his detractors were willing to admit. There is testimony from men who had no motive for advancing his cause that he was more than a military *fanfaron*, more than a 'gifted *condottiere*' (Milyutin)[91] —not, perhaps, a great strategist, but a field commander of the first rank. A German student of the battles around Plevna declared both his offensive and defensive actions to be 'worthy of great consideration and thorough study' and to show 'a rare combination of rashness and prudence'.[92]

[85] T. von Trotha, *Tactical Studies on the Battles around Plevna*, tr. C. Reichmann (Kansas City, 1896), 50, 57; Gazenkampf, *Moi dnevnik* (n. 25), 69–70; E. Trettau, *Kuropatkin und seine Unterführer* (Berlin, 1913), i, 6; A. N. Kuropatkin, *Kritische Rückblicke . . . nach Aufsätzen von Kuropatkin* (Berlin, 1885–90), 7–8.

[86] N. N. Rusanov, *Na rodine, 1859–1882* (M., 1931), 126.

[87] D. I. Ilovaisky, *Melkie sochineniya, stat'i i pis'ma, 1857–1887* (Spb., 1888), 260; Anon., *Russland* (n. 81), 354; Fortunatov, *Voina* (n. 81), 51, 92.

[88] Ibid. 47.

[89] Novikova, *Skobeleff* (n. 1), 109.

[90] Wellesley, op. cit. (n. 18), 35–6; *War Correspondence . . . 'Daily News'* (n. 20), i, 354–9; Herbert, op. cit. (n. 26), 206; F. Stanley, *St. Petersburg to Plevna* (1878), 122–3.

[91] E. M. Feoktistov, *Vospominaniya* (L., 1929), 379.

[92] Trotha, op. cit. (n. 85); C. von Saraux, *Der russisch-türkische Krieg* (Leipzig, 1878), 128; H. M. E. Bunker, *The Story of the Russo–Turkish War in Europe* (1911), *passim*: A. M. Zaionch-

It was only partially his own doing that he came in Russian military thinking to stand for and to justify the tradition that courage and morale counted for more than technology, that the bayonet was mightier than the bullet, and that Russia's superb human material, if inspired by great captains, more than made up for material or numerical inferiority. He had, it is true, said that morale was three times as important as numbers or *matériel*, and that is what was most often remembered.[93] But he had also equipped his division with Peabody–Martini rifles taken from the Turks, because they were better than Russian issue; he urged his soldiers to dig in for protection and insisted that they carry entrenching tools; and he had complained of the superiority of Turkish artillery.[94] He was far from disdaining technical innovation and improved weapons or believing (with Dragomirov and his followers) that taking cover during the attack undermined the soldiers' offensive spirit and went against the Russian grain. That doctrine, which was still practised during the Japanese War and had not entirely died out by 1914, was not Skobelev's, although by the high value he placed on the courage of men and commanders, as well as the importance he attached to personal leadership, he seemed to subscribe to it.[95]

Professional evaluations of Skobelev's performance cannot, however, account for his almost instant popularity during the war. Official telegrams mentioned his name no more frequently or prominently than those of Gurko, Dragomirov, Imeretinsky, Radetsky or Mirsky, and of these, at least Gurko's was widely recognized and honoured. Yet it was Skobelev who was foremost in the public eye, his picture that was most often seen, his exploits that were most often related and turned into legends.[96] There were those who correctly attributed this to the actor in him who was always out to make an impression. 'He valued popularity more than anything and no one was as clever as he in getting it.' When he left for the army on the Danube, he took with him a large number of photographic plates showing him in various poses. Although he did not have an assignment, he was ready if fame should seek him out and prepared to help it along if it should not.[97]

It is true that Skobelev cultivated good relations with the press. Its appetite for news of dramatic events and colourful figures was fed by his vanity and by his energetic pursuit of action. He was keenly aware of the

kovsky, *Nastupatel'nyi boi po opytu deistvii generala Skobeleva* (Spb., 1893); Greene, *Army Life* (n. 81), 126.

[93] Dukmasov, *Vospominaniya* (n. 5), ix; Filippov, *Skobelev* (n. 6), 82; O. F. Geifel'der, 'Vospominaniya', *Russkaya starina*, lii (1886), 399, n. 1.

[94] Furneaux, op. cit. (n. 22), 33; F. V. Greene, *Report on the Russian Army* (New York, 1879), 435; Fortunatov, *Voina* (n. 81), 49–50; Filippov, *Skobelev* (n. 6), 31. Skobelev would not have agreed with the general who said at his funeral: 'Give the peasants axes, put Skobelev at their head and you will have the best army in the world'.

[95] Zaionchkovsky, *Samoderzhavie* (n. 9), 262–5; P. Kenez, 'A Profile of the Pre-Revolutionary Officer Corps', *California Slavic Studies*, vii (1973), 152; A. A. Polivanov, *Iz dnevnikov* (M., 1924), 5–6, 173–4; Apuschkin, *Skobelew* (n. 69), 22; Greene, op. cit. (n. 94), 450–1; Beskrovny, op. cit. (n. 6), 418–19.

[96] *Polnyi sbornik offitsial'nykh telegram vostochnoi voiny, 1887–1878* (Spb., 1878); N. Lanskaya, *Lavry i terny* (Spb., 1884), 16; A. A. Ignat'ev, *50 let v stroyu* (M., 1950), i, 25.

[97] Feoktistov, *Vospominaniya* (n. 91), 379; Vrangel', *Vospominaniya* (n. 13), 136.

role the press could play in bringing him to the notice of the Tsar and the war ministry if his immediate superiors should fail to do so; and he realized its utility in keeping him informed of developments in the field and at headquarters. Reporters moved about more easily than did generals who were tied to their sectors and units; there were occasions when headquarters first learned of the outcome of an engagement through courier services set up by correspondents. There were about eighty of these, as well as artists and photographers. Perhaps a third represented Russian newspapers, the rest French, German, English, Austrian and American publications, with some of them (e.g. Francis Stanley of the *Manchester Guardian* and J. A. MacGahan of the London *Daily News*) writing also for Russian papers.

The press and its correspondents made this the 'breakfast war', one of the most thoroughly covered and eagerly followed of modern wars. It was the last major conflict to have been so fully described. Never again would journalists move with such freedom across the battlefields, take part in the fighting, gain medals or commendations, and receive the first-hand accounts of participants. Skobelev may have been the only Russian general with a command of English; the only one to hold his picture in readiness for the press; the only one to have close personal relations with several correspondents; and the only one who dictated for a London paper the graphic account of an operation for which its correspondent arrived too late.[98]

Certainly, he alone of the Russian generals won the admiration and affection of journalists, although he was not the only one who liked to see his name in the papers or welcomed their representatives.[99] Grand Duke Nikolay had himself agreed that they should not be ignored or offended. The officer whose job it was to deal with them believed that since public opinion had become a force to reckon with, it was better to attempt to dispose the correspondents in one's favour than to antagonize them by restrictions. The weight of public opinion had been recognized in the government before the war began, and the decision to enter it was influenced by that recognition. The interest which press and public took in foreign affairs before the outbreak of hostilities was deepened by the wish of family and friends to learn all they could about their fighting men. Among these, since the introduction of the new service law, there were many who were not professional, long-term soldiers and who had kept up their links with home, and not a few who were literate and recorded their experiences in letters or for publication.[100]

The Russo–Turkish War was indubitably popular in one sense, if in no other: it was followed closely by the populace and it was popularized, that is, made widely accessible, by the public press. Skobelev was a prime beneficiary

---

[98] F. L. Bullard, *Famous War Correspondents* (Boston, 1914), 96–102, 143–54; *War Correspondence . . . 'Daily News'* (n. 20), ii, 21; Furneaux, op. cit. (n. 22), 16; Stanley, *St. Petersburg* (n. 90), 217; Gazenkampf, *Moi dnevnik* (n. 25), *passim*; Nemirovich-Danchenko, *God voiny* (n. 26), iii, 120–22; Greene, *Army Life* (n. 81), 163–7; Wellesley, op. cit. (n. 18), 22–3; Pfeil, *Experiences* (n. 30), 58.

[99] A. E. Kaufman, 'Za kulisami pechati', *Golos minuvshego*, 1914 no. 9, pp. 201–8.

[100] Anon., *Russland* (n. 81), 385–6, 412–13; Fortunatov estimates that half the army consisted of recalled reservists (*Voina* (n. 81), 60).

of that popularity because the character of the press, the needs of the public, and his own character and needs coincided. In that respect the Skobelev phenomenon was unprecedented, almost revolutionary in the Russian context. A man of not especially exalted standing or achievements was carried to the heights of prominence by his own driving will and by the new political awareness of a mass public which had only recently come into being. Pobedonostsev was right when he observed that the lower orders were talking freely (too freely, he thought) of affairs of state, and his view is amply borne out by other evidence.[101]

For those who could not read, there were others who would read to them; there was the talk of streets and bazaars, the illustrated newspapers, the picture cards and the cheap coloured prints depicting scenes of battles. And always there was Skobelev. A. N. Engel'gardt, banished to his estate in Smolensk *guberniya*, wrote in one of his 'Letters from the Village' that the newspaper was uppermost in everyone's mind. The first words of the peasant who came to talk about the harvest or other matters were: 'What is new in the papers? What about Skobelev and Gurko?' Others were eager to know how much land had been taken from the Turks, and whether any of it would be given to the peasants. The master's papers were sent to the kitchen and read out loud. Fedoseich, Ivan, Avdot'ya and Mikhei listened with rapt attention to stories about the White General and always asked beforehand if there was anything 'by the one who writes about Skobelev'.[102]

The son of a lower-class family in St. Petersburg remembered that when news from the front was bad, Skobelev was the one who was expected to put matters right. 'We pictured him as a super-hero, and legends about him were making the rounds.' More than a hero, he was also a human being who treated his soldiers as human beings, would not allow them to be beaten, trusted them and was trusted in return. During the long and perplexing halt before 'Kostipol' it was rumoured that he would enter the city in defiance of orders and dare the English to throw him out.[103]

This was the Skobelev who survived in the popular imagination—eternally young, handsome, victorious, defiant alike of foreign foes and the mean-spirited, fearful grandees who had stood in his way and blocked the realization of Russia's rights and of her people's dreams. This Skobelev was not only a superman, but also very much a real man with a man's failings and the common touch. He was not, of course, the only Skobelev who was remembered. Among the more sophisticated, there was the grand strategist with plans for an invasion of India and war against Germany (the latter supposedly removed from his papers at his death on orders of Alexander III); the patriot of Slavophile sentiment whose few, not very coherent, political comments were offered as a political credo and an endorsement of paternalistic monarchy as the form of government most just and best suited to the large mass of Russia's people.

[101] Ambler, *Russian Journalism* (n. 76), 155; J. Watstein, 'Ivan Sytin', *Russian Review*, xxx (1971), 46; Lanskaya, *Lavry* (n. 96), 16.
[102] Engel'gardt. *Iz derevni* (n. 2), 206, 218–19; Ilya Tolstoy, *Tolstoy, My Father* (Chicago, 1971), 97.
[103] Popov, *Minuvshee* (n. 82), 29–31.

Fundamentally, however, the educated conservatives who tried to make Skobelev the instrument for the propagation of a conservative yet popular monarchism saw or represented him after his death in much the same way as did the masses: as a symbol of national unity and commonly shared purpose, of bold leadership and awesome power combined with fatherly concern —in short, a surrogate for the tsar who no longer embodied these qualities.

Beginning with the latter part of Alexander II's reign, conservative monarchists from Ivan Aksakov to Lev Tikhomirov—proponents of a truly national autocracy based on the union of tsar and people—deplored the ruler's abandonment of the traditions of autocracy. More or less discreetly, they complained that the Tsar had allowed himself to be isolated behind a bureaucratic wall or that he had made concessions to the pernicious principles of Western liberalism and tolerated the exploitation of his people by a selfish capitalism of foreign origin. All this, as well as certain personal failings and weaknesses of the ruler, they saw as the cause of the people's waning attachment to the autocracy and of its feeble defence of national interests at home and abroad. By 1904 Tikhomirov had come around to the view that the salvation of monarchism in Russia might require the destruction of the monarchy. 'There have been neither ministers nor an Emperor for a long time, only pale shadows of the past.'[104] Skobelev, as the author of an article entitled 'The Last Hero' put it in 1912, was that rare phenomenon, the national leader (narodnyi vozhd'), who alone is capable of setting a nation's course in new directions. 'After our royal leaders Peter and Catherine, he was the most powerful personality of that type to appear in Russian history.'[105]

The feeling, which was close to despair, that the tsar was no longer the visible and vital defender of tsarism, led to the search for others to carry its banner. The search was complicated by the realization, at least on the part of conservatives who did not totally delude themselves, that their cause had few advocates who could gain the affection or even the ear of the nation. There was a constant and plaintive refrain: we are drowned by the opposition; we have few articulate spokesmen, no popular figures. As early as 1856 Ivan Aksakov was grieved to find that Belinsky was read by everyone in the provinces, but the Slavophiles hardly at all. In 1880 Dostoevsky wrote to his wife that he had to speak at the Pushkin memorial because he was the only one 'of our whole party, our whole idea' to whom people would listen. They had tired of Aksakov, and the rest were without weight. In 1913 a right-wing supporter of a strong monarchy admitted: 'We are as rare as the aurochs'.[106]

In Skobelev, those who felt that the monarchy needed a popular champion thought they had found their man, the idol for which, as the German ambassador wrote, the army and the country yearned. But when he died, all too soon, their lamentations began again—that some kind of curse

[104] See H. Rogger, 'Reflections on Russian Conservatism', Jahrbücher für Geschichte Osteuropas, xiv (1966), 195–212, and 'The Beilis Case', Slavic Review, xxv (1966), 622.

[105] P. Pertsov, 'Poslednii geroi', Novoe vremya, 24 June 1912; Ditmar, op. cit. (n. 8), 166.

[106] I. S. Aksakov v ego pis'makh, iii (M., 1892), 290–1; Dostoevsky, Pis'ma, iv (M., 1959), 157; see also n. 104 above.

afflicted Russia, that all her most talented sons were fated to die before their time, that only mediocrities remained.[107]

Ironically, Skobelev's death was a blessing for the votaries of his cult: not only was it difficult to reconcile the idea of autocracy with the presence of a surrogate monarch, but also Russia's last two tsars—and Nicholas more so than his father—were inordinately sensitive to any diminution of their prestige and primacy. A live, charismatic, vocal Skobelev, a successful general with a following in the army, among the masses, and among segments of privileged society would have been difficult to tolerate. A dead Skobelev, on the other hand, posed no great problem and could be claimed as an adornment and pillar of the existing order. His biography could safely be authorized for school use, his monument at last dedicated (in Moscow in 1912), his name and example invoked in two wars to inspire patriotism and military prowess.[108] More than once the opinion was expressed during and after the war against Japan that Russia would have prevailed if her armies had been led by Skobelev. The appointment of Kuropatkin as commander-in-chief was due in large measure to the belief that he had inherited the aura and the secret of victory from the man whose chief-of-staff he had been in happier campaigns. The white horse presented to Kuropatkin by the citizens of Moscow when he departed for the Far East was the naïve expression of that belief; the sceptical question of General Dragomirov was its denial and, at the same time, a tribute to the man who had inspired it. 'Who', Dragomirov asked, 'will be Kuropatkin's Skobelev?'[109]

The adoption of Skobelev as a patron saint of official nationalism obscured the historical meaning of the Skobelev phenomenon. It represented, in a confused and unconscious way, a groping for a non-dynastic nationalism, a way for conservatives to break out of the isolation to which, until its end, the monarchy condemned them. Even after 1905, when they were free—in fact, compelled by circumstances—to participate in the political contest and to seek a mass basis, conservatives were inhibited by the incubus of the monarchy and their attachment to it. It is not likely that Skobelev, had he lived, could have led them out of their isolation without adopting a broader, a more dynamic and inclusive vision of nationalism than they were willing to embrace. The survival of the Skobelev cult, with all its ambiguities, reflects the predicament faced by conservative nationalism in its futile efforts to escape from that predicament by a change of personalities rather than of principles.

[107] H. L. von Schweinitz, *Briefwechsel* (Berlin, 1928), 366; Tyutcheva, op. cit. (n. 53), 233; Aksakov, *Sochineniya* (n. 40), v, 654; Vollan, op. cit. (n. 59), 131–3.

[108] Shavel'sky, *Vospominaniya* (n. 4), 18, 37; Polivanov, *Iz dnevnikov* (n. 95), 160–1; Apuschkin, *Skobelew* (n. 69); I. P. Yuvachev, 'Voina i vera', *Ist. vestnik*, cxxxix (1915), 566–90; 'Voina i legendy', leaflet of 1904 in Columbia Russian Archives. At the time of the Bosnian crisis an Englishman wrote of Skobelev: 'Had he been living today, it is probable that Austria would have thought twice and even thrice before her determination to tear up the Berlin treaty. . . .' (W. T. Stead, *ed.*, *The M.P. for Russia. Reminiscences and Correspondence of Olga Novikoff* (1909), ii, 176).

[109] Ditmar, op. cit. (n. 8), 158; *Peterburgskaya gazeta*, 24 June 1911; *Birzhevye vedomosti*, 24 June 1912; Vrangel', *Vospominaniya* (n. 13), 175; L. Tikhomirov, '25 let nazad', *Krasnyi arkhiv*, xxxviii (1930), 40.

Skobelev had recognized that an old régime and its defenders could no more maintain themselves in the modern world without some understanding and support from society than an army with antiquated weapons could hope to defeat a technically superior foe. Russian politics, like military technology, had to be brought up to date. When he learned that Alexander III might appoint his uncle Adlerberg minister of foreign affairs, Skobelev protested that for all his excellent qualities the Count was not a politician (*politik*) but a diplomatist of the old school, with too high a regard for dynastic considerations and for the secrets of the cabinet. Confronted by the modern politician, the old-fashioned diplomatist was in much the same position as the Russian soldier with his flint-lock had been in the Crimean War when he faced an adversary armed with Enfield rifles.

Only a politician is ⸺able of recognizing the full necessity for a broad, public airing of national, political, and social questions before today's nervous, capricious, highly suspicious thinking majority in Europe and even in Russia. Finally, only a politician will appreciate the irresistible power of the printed word and, valuing and respecting the rightful public role of the press, will carry it with him in the name of the great goals which, ultimately, state and society share. . . . Cavour, Garibaldi, Gambetta, Bismarck, Beaconsfield, Gladstone, Midhat Pasha, they are the typical contemporary politicians. How colourless Beust, Shuvalov, even Gorchakov . . . appear in comparison.[110]

Skobelev was anything but colourless; but without a political arena, movement, and programme, without a crowned ally or a firm purpose, he was—and would have remained—as ineffective as the traditional bureaucrats he blamed for Russia's weaknesses and troubles.

[110] Quoted by Nemirovich–Danchenko, *Skobelev* (n. 12), ii, 147–8.

Nevill Forbes, 1883–1929:
Some Family Letters from Russia

By FELICITY ASHBEE

THE name of Nevill Forbes, Reader and, later, Professor of Russian at Oxford from 1910 to 1929, was more or less synonymous with Russian language studies in England between the wars. Generations of learners of the language were brought up on his four *Russian Books* (issued during the First World War and frequently reprinted), and on his *Russian Grammar* and *Elementary Russian Grammar*, published in 1914 and 1919 and reissued in revised editions by Professors Dumbreck and Hill in 1964 and 1943 respectively.

Nevill Forbes was, however, much more than just a grammarian. He was widely travelled, a keen observer, an excellent letter-writer (as we shall see), a sensitive and gifted musician, and a cultivated and humane man. He was very fond of children (he translated Russian children's books which were illustrated by his cousin, Valery Karrik), and he certainly possessed remarkable qualities as an uncle—as a niece can testify.

Two factors propelled my uncle towards Russia. The first—family connexions with the country—was almost normal among early teachers of Russian in England. The second—the tuberculosis from which he suffered from the age of seventeen to about twenty—provided an unusual but powerful impulse towards Russia, and specifically to the sanatorium which his mother's brother, George Carrick, had established in the 1870s near Anatol'evka in the steppes about forty kilometres NNW. of Orenburg.[1] It appears (as 'Dzhanetovka') on a Soviet map of 1957.

Nevill's mother, Jessie Carrick, was born in Cronstadt of a Scots family in the timber trade. An attractive and mercurial personality, she was brought up entirely in St. Petersburg except for two years from the age of fifteen to seventeen which she spent at a boarding school in Edinburgh. While on a fortnight's holiday from school at a Yorkshire spa, she made friends with a fourteen-year-old boy, Frank Forbes, who had been sent there for his asthma. A correspondence (which she initiated) began: it continued until ten years later Frank went to St. Petersburg, married her in the Embassy Chapel, and brought her back to share his life in the stockbroker-belt at Sevenoaks in Kent.

But if Jessie was hardly an average Victorian young lady, neither was Frank the typical Victorian stockbroker. His hard-working Scots father had insisted that both his sons should possess not only the manners of gentlemen but also a sound understanding of business values, and to this end each had

[1] See Brockhaus-Efron, *Entsiklopedicheskii slovar'*, xvii (1896), 19.

been sent to Geneva for two years—whence they returned fluent in French and German, and accomplished musicians.

Jessie had a lovely singing voice; evenings with song and chamber music became part of the pattern of the young Forbes ménage, and when their children were born (Janet in 1877, and Nevill on 19 February 1883), music and foreign languages were a natural part of their environment.

A German governess (who, in the sound Russian tradition, continued to be looked after by the family until her death) had sole charge of the children's upbringing, until Nevill, at about the age of nine, was sent as a weekly boarder to a local preparatory school. Here Latin, Greek, and Spanish were added to his languages and he studied the piano and the cello.

Early photographs show him as a sad and rather delicate-looking little boy (his unusual shortsightedness was not diagnosed until he was about ten years old). He nevertheless seems to have done all the normal boyish things, collecting caterpillars and stamps, even tolerating football, though he was perhaps more than usually sensitive to nature.

A letter written to his sister when he was ten runs:

My report is good, and the only thing I am shaky in is arithmetic. . . . Greek = I'm top. Latin = I'm 4th from top. French = I've been top for 3 weeks!! English = I'm top. Music getting on splendidly. . . . Today has been beautiful. I am doing the 3rd prop: in Euclid. The leaves are falling fast and soon we shall be preparing for the bonfire, fireworks etc.

In 1893, when Janet was fifteen and a half, she was sent (chaperoned by the devoted governess) to Berlin for a year to study German and music, and Nevill and his mother went over to join her for Christmas. Mrs. Forbes went on alone to celebrate a nostalgic and hectic New Year in St. Petersburg, leaving Nevill with his sister. He sat in on her music and gymnastic lessons, and together they went to a number of concerts, skated on the frozen Wannsee, and talked a great deal of German.

Christmas 1894 saw another family reunion, this time in Paris, where Janet was continuing her education with a year in France, lodging (still chaperoned!) with an extremely bohemian opera-singing family. This was Nevill's initiation into the French capital and the delights of opera.

In the following year he was seriously ill, with measles in the spring, and an attack of typhoid in the autumn which caused him to miss school for an entire term. During these illnesses his mother nursed him with a devotion and competence surprising in one who was somewhat disorganized by nature; her solicitousness inevitably made for an intimacy of relationship which was perhaps decisive for his whole later development. After so prolonged a convalescence it must have been difficult indeed for him to assert the normal independence of a thirteen-year-old, especially when faced with such a dominating and unpredictable personality as his mother. But the bond between himself and his sister helped, and letters show that he opened his heart to her and that, in spite of their five-year difference in age, they greatly enjoyed each other's company.

In the summer of 1896 there was a wonderful fortnight of Wagner at

Bayreuth with his mother and sister, and in January of the following year his life as a public school boy at Marlborough began.

Only a couple of letters survive from the Marlborough years. In one of these, written to his father in July 1898 when he was fifteen, he alluded to his hopes of getting into the diplomatic service:

From what you may have heard, from Janet perhaps, and from me some time ago, you must see clearly that my thoughts have all along tended towards Diplomacy and politics. . . . To obtain a position in the Diplomatic Service is no doubt *hard* but obviously *not impossible*. Next holidays I intend seriously studying Spanish, and with additional possibilities of French, German, and Russian happily afforded me, you will quite see that it doesn't seem at all hopeless to go in for it.

In September 1898 his sister married C. R. Ashbee,[2] and a letter written to her in March 1899—headed 'Private'—gives some indication of how her marriage must have seemed to him like the ending of an epoch:

Many thanks for your last letter, the extatic part of which I confess I don't understand! But as I am quite determined at present at any rate, to remain unmarried all my life, I fear I shan't be able to sympathize with you! And yet, I sometimes wish that I (whether older like you, or younger as I now am) had someone who was as myself, a part of me, with whom I had all thought in common, and from whom I should hide nothing! The world, at least this part of it, and I are so mutually unsympathetic, that I feel sure I am out of place, so to speak: Perhaps it is rather unfair to say that, but at least it is so full of *artificialism* and hypocrisy, and vice, and all sorts of awful things, that I sometimes feel very strange. I can scarcely say lonely, because I know I have always *you*, who are reasonable and helpful. . . . Not that I can complain of my own personal comfort or actual momentary happiness, but I envy you and Charlie, so wrapt up in each other, so happy, mutual and perfected, indeed I do! And yet I fear it can never be so with me.

This letter perhaps shows no more than a sensitive and intelligent sixteen-year-old voicing his doubts and self-searchings, but before he had a chance to resolve his problems for himself, illness struck again. In the spring of 1900 tuberculosis was diagnosed. Instinctively, his mother turned to her doctor brother, George Carrick.

When Jessie Carrick had left Russia on her marriage, her two brothers and her mother (her father was already dead) had stayed behind. The older brother, William, was a talented photographer (and the father of the artist, Valery Karrik); the younger, George, who had studied medicine at St. Andrews, was, among other things, one of the Embassy doctors.

Nevill had met his Uncle George on various occasions. Probably the first time he really remembered him was in 1887, when George (already the author of a book on the koumiss treatment of tuberculosis)[3] had come to London to attend an exhibition with a demonstration herd of Tatar mares.

---

[2] See *Dictionary of National Biography, 1941–1950* (1959), 21–2.
[3] *Koumiss, or Fermented Mare's Milk, and its Uses in the Treatment and Cure of Pulmonary Consumption and Other Wasting Diseases* (Edinburgh and London, 1881).

George Carrick had been an unconventional doctor from the moment when he qualified and returned to Russia from Scotland in 1864. He had good looks, a fine figure, and bachelor status; and his Russo–Scots command over the bottle, though it had sometimes lost him patients, had also got him out of many a difficulty. During his mother's lifetime he had wanted to experiment with the fermented mares' milk treatment of tuberculosis, and had made several fact-finding forays to the Samara region in this connexion. But only after her death in 1876 did he start seriously in the field.

He called his sanatorium 'Dzhanetovka' (see Plates Ic, II–III) after his niece, Nevill's sister, and when the threat of consumption threw its shadow over the Forbes family, it seemed obvious that Nevill should go to his doctor uncle for treatment. He and his mother set off for Orenburg in May 1900.

The transition from the Victorian Gothic mansion at Sevenoaks and the public school routine at Marlborough to the hutted encampment in the middle of the steppes, must have been traumatic, and though Nevill did not realize it immediately, it was probably to be the decisive factor in changing the course of his life.

Treatment consisted of living quietly for the summer months in the Sanatorium compound, drinking koumiss (the quantity varied according to the patient and the nature and state of his disease) and taking exercise both on horseback and on foot. In his book George Carrick stressed that though koumiss could be helpful when drunk elsewhere, the steppes themselves had an important part to play; partly because the vegetation there conditioned the quality of the mares' milk and its fermentation, and (perhaps equally important in view of the ideas then current about tuberculosis) because, during the summer months, there was 'a complete absence of dewfall at sunset . . . the grass is in fact as dry in the steppes several hours after sunset as it is during the day; while the dew commences falling thickly, and the air feels very fresh and even chilly only about an hour or two before sunrise.' In the opinion of the day, this was very helpful for those with any disease of the lungs or respiratory passages.

So Nevill read what books he had brought with him (he mentions reading Thackeray's *Henry Esmond* for the second time, Goethe's *Faust*, and a volume of German poetry), played the piano a great deal, had daily Russian lessons, and rode out on the empty steppes sometimes with another patient, often, quite happily, alone. On 28 June he wrote his sister:

I have taken quite lately 4 bottles of Koumiss a day, but now that the weather is much cooler, no one takes so much, and I have fallen back on 3 or 3½ till it gets hot again. But I am afraid I never really enjoy it, as some people do, or say they do, but try to get down as much as possible. Uncle George has had a kirgiz kibitka or tent put up for me to sleep in, which I shan't do till it gets drier and warmer! It consists of a framework of wooden lattice about 5 feet high (round) and then a sort of dome! like this [drawing]. It is then covered with once white sheeps' wool felt, and bound round with numerous cords. The top part undoes, and is pulled back by a cord, so you get the air in that way. The low door is curiously carved and painted In white, blue, green and red. I shall feel like a tramp when inside!

(a)   (b)

(c)

PLATE I. (a) Nevill Forbes with his parents and sister (1897).   (b) Nevill Forbes (1900).
(c) Dzhanetovka (1883).

(a)

(b)

PLATE II. (a) Dzhanetovka (1889; Dr. Carrick standing fourth from the left in the back
row). (b) Dzhanetovka: the dining-room.

(a)

(b)

PLATE III.   (a) Dzhanetovka: a patient's hut.   (b) Dzhanetovka: mare-milking.

(a)

While there we visited a most curious village swing: a huge affair
about 50 ft high, like this:

of a most complic-
ated design, but
strongly, tho' roughly
built.

You see the 4 swinging seats.
The whole frame was kept swinging
right round, like the Big Wheel, on
on a small scale, by the villagers.

(b)

PLATE IV.   (a) At the fair at Anatol'evka (1900).   (b) From a letter of 9 August 1900.

In a letter of 11 July he wrote:

There are here, besides Mr. Bergomier and Mr. Steinberg the violinist, whom I like very much, exactly 7 people who can speak any language but their own with any fluency! And you may rest assured that I shall not ever be likely to miss an opportunity of in any way benefitting myself by them. . . . This wonderful empire is really an extraordinary thing! Its vast distances, enormous population and extent, all under the absolute control of a handful of men at Petersburg! And so completely kept under control! Huge, though absurdly built railways, stretching out in all directions; I say absurd, for they make idiotic semicircles and huge curling embankments where they are quite unnecessary, and which prohibit any approach to high speed. They also foolishly make them single line, when considering the cheapness of land, and also for political reasons, they ought certainly to be double. Next year they begin making one from Orenburg to Tashkent direct, which will threaten our frontiers, bringing Petersburg in direct communication with the Pamirs! . . . The other day I and Mr. Bergomier with some other Russians who drove, rode to a village 7 miles off at 7 a.m. for the blessing of the wood, with which they are building a new church, having already a month ago blessed the stone of which the foundation is built! The half hour service was held in a very small and stuffy old church, where we had to stand with swarms of peasants, the whole time, in a broiling day! We were somewhat relieved when the incense came round! and still more so when we got out, though the ceremony was very interesting. A curious thing is that the priest administers the communion in a spoon to all the infants of the village, held in their mothers' arms and screaming vociferously! The number was quite astonishing. Then we had to stand another hour in the new church, the walls of which were not half built and *uncovered* in the roasting sun! while water was sprinkled on the wood etc: Altogether most interesting! The women in their many coloured cottons, and the men charmingly though quietly dressed in cloth or velveteen: long coat with full skirt, open large coloured short sleeves, embroidered neck and knickerbockers and top boots.

On 9 August he wrote:

On Sunday Mother and some others drove in the large carriage to Anatolyvka after lunch, and I followed with Olga A's nephew on horseback. . . . While there we visited a most curious village swing: a huge affair about 20 ft. high like this [see Plate IV] of a most complicated design but strongly tho' roughly built. You see the 4 swinging seats. The whole frame was kept swinging *right round*, like the Big Wheel, on a small scale, by the villagers. It was altogether most amusing. We later had tea in the house of the Starost, or chief villager, where 3 daughters in law lived together *and peaceably!!* *with* three husbands and many children. The next day we kept Mother's birthday, and as it is here the custom to congratulate not only the one person but all the relatives, all rose from their seats, the band played a special piece culminating in a grand crash simultaneously with loud hurrahs, and all shook hands with me! We had a warm time of it! . . . in the evening we all had cruchon [i.e. champagne-cup] for dinner and some danced after, Uncle G. doing a polka with Mother! Then came the servants who greatly enjoyed it and their national dances especially, the band playing the whole time: we eventually got to bed at 11.45 p.m.! Several people are leaving this week, and but few will stay on till the end I fear.

He wrote his last letter to his sister on 21 August:

We are now only 23 patients including Uncle G., a lady housekeeper and son, and Mother; tomorrow 17 only. . . . I think we shall stay till quite the end if the weather keeps fine, as we have now finally decided to travel straight through by train to Petersburg, via Samara and Moscow. We shall probably arrive (at St. Petersburg) about the 6th or 7th Sept: perhaps later, and shall spend *at least* a week at Auntie Carrick's [the widow of the photographer uncle, William]. . . . I should like to catch the weekly Siberian express at Samara, but it is difficult to arrange. . . . The autumn is beginning here already, and the poplars round the dining room are turning yellow. The harvest is in full swing and the endless fields on the other side of the river are dotted over with sheaves of splendid wheat. It is such a different scene from our little hedged English meadows; here we can see the downs for a length of about 10 miles covered with sheaves! For winnowing they simply harness two horses to a large rolling stone, and then they drag it about in a round space over the ears of corn. The clouds here on a fine day are simply magnificent, one can see such an enormous expanse of sky. We shall be very sorry to leave the place, it is so peaceful and absolutely removed from any idea of turmoil or railways.

With a wonderful faith in the reliability of international and English time-tables, he added that they would be going direct 'from St. P, via Flushing, and taking slow trains via Swanley to Kemsing to get home by lunchtime'.

But in spite of George Carrick's belief in the koumiss treatment, when Nevill returned to England the specialists advised Switzerland for the winter, and by November he was installed in a much less interesting sanatorium in Caux. Only the arrival of a Miss Baird in February relieved the boredom, and he spent his eighteenth birthday 'very happily lugeing down to Montreux' with her. Miss Baird's elder brother was in the diplomatic service in Cairo, and Nevill wrote to Janet:

She gives me plenty of hints about it. She says Russian is *the* language, and shorthand, typewriting, international law, are all most useful and esteemed subjects, and that shooting and riding are indispensable as well as dancing, conversational discretion, etc., etc. Her sister and father Sir Alexander Baird arrive tomorrow, and they stay long, and she tells me to pump him, and get him to interest himself in me. . . . It often seems to me that father is not very keen about my going in for it; he never speaks to me about it, and yet never mentions any other career I might take up! If he does not wish it, why has he silently encouraged me so far? I can't understand it at all! And then he proposes for me to go to Australia next winter! . . . but ought I not, since I am now practically well, to go and learn German or Russian at Berlin or Moscow, both fairly healthy places, or the Krimea if you like, *the* place for delicate people in winter? . . . Don't you yourself think I ought to devote the precious time to perfecting my languages? . . . I suppose Uncle George is urging my going to Orenburg again: I don't think it would be any good unless I could stipulate for a course of regular Russian lessons.

All now depended on the second specialist's opinion (he was to see him in May). At the end of March he wrote:

Now I am in high hopes about Oxford, since as you will have heard, Tucker-Wise pronounces me quite cured!! I only trust Powell will do the same. . . . But of course if he decides on Orenburg again it puts off Oxford indefinitely, for getting back thence in mid-September I should not have time to work up for my exam. . . . I am most anxious to get it all settled, as you can imagine.

But apparently the specialists did not agree, Uncle George's counsels won the day, and Nevill and his mother set off for another summer at Orenburg, to be followed by a winter (1901–2) in the Caucasus and Crimea after Dzhanetovka closed.

The letters from this second stay give an interesting indication of the extent to which this part of the Russian Empire was still oriental (whether Islamic or Buddhist) or 'heathen'.

The 'Mohamedan equivalent of baptism' of the baby of one of the Sanatorium's Tatar women prompted a long letter to Janet on 8 August 1901:

Three Mullahs came from the neighbouring townlet of Imangolova and they, with all the grown-up males of the family, sat round 3 sides of the room (on the floor, à la Turque) and the principle Mullah, a handsome old man, with the baby smothered in clothes lying on the ground in front of him, sang a long chant in E minor for about 10 minutes. Curious sort of beginningless and endless Gregorian tunes only on E, F♯, G, A and B in 6 time. After that they all drew their palms quietly over their faces and then took away the baby. Then they brought two enormous dishes, one containing huge fat lumps of mutton, the other a number of tiny thin pastry things, each about the size of a penny, which we had seen being made by the woman (none of whom attended the ceremony) in their tent. Then they all gobbled with their hands as forks, and it seemed the correct thing for anyone, finding an unusually choice morsel, to thrust it into the mouth of his neighbour or host, so that nobody fed himself!!! The younger Mullah, by name Sherafydyn Tugan invited us to go and see them on Friday, their holy day: so accordingly on that day, after lunch, we hired 5 horses from the village, and took two of Uncle George's carriages, one a simple basket on poles, and the other a 'dolgushka', in which the people sit along the sides back to back, their feet dangling down on to the board near the ground. I drove this equipage with 3 steeds! In it were Mother, and a lady and two boys at her table, in the other an officer (who drove a pair) and his wife and another lady. . . . I was rather nervous to begin with, but soon got into it, and as here there is no difficulty about breadth of road when you meet another carriage, and nothing, not even a stone, for any horse to shy at, I managed all right, and didn't have any mishap. We had tea in the house of the Mullah, and all sat round the room on the floor and had a long piece of red linen rolled out on our knees as a Table Cloth! The samovar was put on the floor, and we were regaled with bread, eggs (minus cups or spoons!) and black currants fresh and preserved!

His old parents were present, and his wife made her appearance after the dismissal of her brother-in-law from the room! Also a sweet little girl with bare feet and a graceful sweeping dress of lilac cotton, and a gala embroidered cap the shape of a Liberty cap, only black and gold, and a breastplate of embroidery and silver coins on her chest, fastened onto the dress like a bib.

The Tartar dwellings are incomparably cleaner than the Russian peasant huts. Afterwards we visited the little wooden mosque which consists of three absolutely bare rooms, one larger than another. In the last there is a small alcove for the priest to stand in, and some steps at the top of which he preaches. We clomb up to the tower from whence he cries to the people five times a day, and got home in time for dinner.

Surviving letters after the final departure from Dzhanetovka are from Astrakhan', Kislovodsk and Yalta, some of them written on board the boats which served his mother and himself as hotels. He wrote from Astrakhan' on 3 September:

We arrived here today at 1 p.m. after a peaceful night, the wind having mercifully gone down. From Tzaritzin to Astrakhan the river is much broader and the whole morning we were cutting thro' an immense looking glass about 2 miles broad, with on either side red dunes or willow forest; a glorious and mind-expanding scene, though scarcely exciting! We passed several curious Buddhist temples of the Kalmik Tartars, built much in the style of the Chinese pagoda. We go half an hour by steamer to their principal colony near here. We are spending tonight on this steamer which doesn't leave for Nizhni again till tomorrow, and we shall spend Wednesday and Thursday nights on the small steamer which will take us on Friday to the big steamer at sea, beyond the mouth of the Volga, and 70 miles from here.

Astrakhan may be called the Russian Venice; although of 130,000 inhabitants, there is as yet no railway, and all communication except in winter, is by water. The length of the quay is very great, and the number of barges, steamers, tugs, and fishing vessels appalling. At night, as now, it is very pretty to see it all lit up and there is a continual chorus of the various shrieks of the steamers, some slowly puffing along with naphtha-filled barges, others, little ones, darting about from one side of the river to the other. In between are many rowing boats laden high with orange and green melons and arbuzes and red tomatoes. Most of the loading and unloading of the steamers and barges is done by Persians, picturesque in their white and coloured clothes and round skull caps, lined with fur and embroidered outside.

The town itself is considerably better than Samara or Orenburg, though also dusty and damp at night. It has an interesting old cathedral and remains of an old Tartar walled citadel, as at Kazan, Nizhni, and Moscow. On the steamer we made, amongst others, the acquaintance of two young Khans of Baku, who told us a lot about the place and advised us, as well as many others, *not* to go into Turkestan, i.e. Samarkand etc., as all those places are subject to most virulent and even mortal malaria! So we shall content ourselves with going to Derbent and Baku, both on the Kaspian, and then by train to Tiflis and on.

Wednesday evening. We have transported ourselves and our baggage onto the smaller steamer that plies between here and the sea, and having secured a good cabin and permission to live here till Friday (when we leave for Petrovsk) are writing in the cosy little saloon, to the accompaniment of the songs of the Persian workmen unloading the cargo of cotton, carpets, etc., etc. I am glad to say we are both perfectly well and happy, and the weather is superb and we both have enormous appetites!! Today we went by a small steamer to the Kalmuck village on the opposite bank and about 4 miles higher up the river. We learnt on the way of some wonderful mud bath Kurort 20 minutes drive from there, and having arrived drove away 5 miles in a rickety cart across the desert, and after being nearly shaken to nothing arrived at a smiling Oasis on the banks of a small chalky blue lake, with a pinky white border, the salt lake from which they take the awful sulphorous black mud for the baths! It was the end of the season and only a few patients were there. It was very much in the style of 'Janetovka' only all the people live in rooms in one large house. It was not nearly as clean as Uncle George's, and more altogether, and not so scattered.

We walked as far as we could on the coating of salt and could feel the quick-sandy mud underneath, and smelt the awful sulphorous smell! On our way back we looked into a Kibitka or wicker round, felt-covered hut of some rich Kalmuck, owner of 2,000 horses. The husband was away but the wife received us very seriously, with a nephew and two nieces, all dressed in queer native constructional dresses, and sort of mitres covered with red silk and cloth of gold. Their type is absolutely Chinese, and they are almost all Buddhist. Their coal black hair is parted in the middle all the way down to their necks and the tresses collected into black silk long thin tubes, hanging down in front and at the end of which are fixed long silver bobbles of various designs!! Their hats are thus [drawing]. In their tent full of magnificent Persian carpets and embroideries, what should I see but a splendid Cleveland bicycle!! the property of the husband. We gave them grapes and sweets, but they took it all very seriously and scarcely smiled or spoke a word!

The next day he wrote again:

We have had another most interesting and successful day in fine and cool weather. We were visited last night by large numbers of flat brown cockroaches, large and small, but managed happily to keep them at bay with frequent doses of insect powder, though we saw them poking their heads out at us from between the chinks! Nevertheless we had a good night. We took a small steamer early to the Kalmuck village and though the head priest was again absent, we got hold of an official and he got the under priest to show us over the temple, though not knowing Russian he could not explain it all to us. The outside is painted all white, beams picked out in blue, green, yellow, and a tall thing on top, surmounted by a sun and moon, gilt. The walls were covered with round and square paintings in blue, green and gold, and the ceiling inside was blue with the whole universe painted on it. Inside was a plain square room, the walls of which were covered with paintings and Kakumonas, all Chinese, of idols in red and blue and gold, most beautifully done. In a little alcove was a large chest full of dovecots in each of which sat a little idol all decked out in yellow! The whole surmounted by a large idol of Buddha. In front was a large round table covered with little silver cups and vases filled with different kinds of bread, given at intervals to, so to speak, communicants. Round the table on sticks were hung curious embroidered things like boots, I don't know *what* for! On beams all round the room hung long things of many pieces of varicoloured silk; for ornament, they said! In two corners stood two boxes bearing large white shells into which they blow and on the boxes were painted the holy yellow dogs with furious eyes and manes!! . . . The Kalmucks themselves are very well educated, far above any other Tartars. One old man with whom we spoke asked us why we did not join England and Ireland by a tunnel, and mentioned the names 'Thames Tunnel', 'La Manche', and 'Pas de Calais'!!!! They are all most picturesquely dressed in flowing dresses of scarlet, crimson, blue or bright yellow, and many men have lovely silver belts.

They are the most interesting thing I have seen for a long time and I would not have missed it for anything.

We went later across the river to see the fish cleaned and salted in one of the principal salting establishments. It may be called the staple industry of the place, in winter and summer, as the numerous salt lakes in the neighbourhood afford great opportunities. The smell at first was appalling but we got used to it! After cleaning them, the women, all in sort of trousers, smother them in salt and fling them by the dozen into enormous cellars filled with brine where they soak for a week before being packed up in barrels and sent off. . . .

Then we visited the Cathedral inside the Kremlin wall; it is very old and quite different from most Russian churches, smaller, very lofty, and thinner cupolas, and various beautiful designs on the walls. The whole painted white and the cupola roofs (5) green. The belfry, a tower standing apart as in all Russian Towns, fell down about 2 years ago and has not been re-built, and looks melancholy piled up in square blocks of bricks. The interior was nothing very wonderful, the only interesting thing being an enormous gold screen about 100 ft high containing 125 large painted images of saints.

By October he was writing from Kislovodsk:

We have spent a very happy month here and shall be sorry to leave next Sat. for Yalta. We have been putting off our departure . . . the weather is so glorious, and we have got to feel so at home here . . . [but] the Pension closes on 14th. . . . It would be pleasanter but for . . . an uneasy feeling when talking about anything except local matters!! The principal and perpetual topics here are naphtha, the all-absorbing Armenians who are a thorn in the Russians' sides, as by their cleverness and enormous capital they dominate Kaukasian affairs, having in their power almost all Tiflis and Baku.

The festivities in France sent everyone into extasies, and they all seem to think the immediate downfall of England certain!![4]

McKinley's death was terrible and I don't see what the Anarchists gain by it, unless Roosevelt is supposed to be more favourable to them?[5] But having done this the Anarchists will probably lose their last place of refuge, as I should think it certain that stricter laws will be introduced against them. . . .

We are fascinated by the charming Kaukasians in their graceful orange, gray or white coats, made down to below the knee, and their swinging figures and flashing daggers and swords!

There are only two letters from Yalta during the autumn of 1901, and they are the last of any that can be called consecutive. He wrote on 22 October 1901:

The quay swarms with 'spider-shops' of all kinds, we are getting quite tired of Persian carpets and Kaukasian belts!!! . . . The people here are not nearly as interesting as in the Kaukasus. They consist mostly of Turks in red fezzes and white or brown or blue coarse linen shirts and extraordinary trousers, bulging above and quite tight below, and with red or green waistbands. There are also many more Russian peasants than at Kislovodsk. They all use brooms for street or house cleaning, of that spiky gorse-like stuff, rare in England, called Butcher's broom, and when I asked a Russian

[4] The Tsar and Tsarina were on a state visit to France from 18 to 21 September 1901.
[5] The United States President was shot on 6 September; he died eight days later.

street sweeper if they were good brooms he said: 'Yes, you won't find such brooms in *Russia*'!!!! And in the Kaukasus when going north, they always say: 'We're going to Russia', or 'When were you last in Russia?' Among the lodgers here are two very interesting men of the Tcheremezi tribe; this tribe, with 2 others, the Tchuvash and Mardva, have always inhabited the Nizhni Novgorod, Simbirsk, Kazan and Ufa Governments, and were all, and are for the most part still, heathens. They worship the evil spirit, having no temples, but bringing all kinds of offerings and praying and sacrificing at oak trees. All 3 tribes have absolutely different languages, and these again are different from any others, but the people, as is evident by the yellow skins, hollow cheeks and coal-black eyes and hair of these two, must be of Mongol origin, I should say.

These two men, educated in Russian schools, and speaking Russian perfectly, always speak their own language amongst themselves, and they, as well as many of their tribesmen, are Christians.

But there are references, too, to more general topics. 'We ought to arrange for a railway into Afghanistan', he wrote, 'but I suppose we shall go on sleeping till the last moment and then find it too late!' And again: 'I think another main cause of our waning trade is in the lack of adaptability of traders or manufacturers and their agents, to the demands and tastes, especially the latter, of their foreign markets.'

His mother's and his stay in the Crimea was, however, typical of that of many health-seekers. They lived in a pension off the high road to Livadia and Sevastopol', while some friends were in a flat only three minutes walk away:

We can see each other distinctly from our balconies. They have a lovely ½ grand Blüthner and have given me a standing invitation to come and play whenever and for as long as I like. . . . The glorious blue-green sea, white foaming, and the high peaceful mountains half covered with Scotch firs, and between the two, the sparkling white town with cupolas in gold and plentiful foliage and gardens, form a lovely picture.

They did not return to England until the spring of 1902.

Whether or not it was Dzhanetovka's koumiss that cured him, Nevill never suffered any recurrence of the tuberculosis, though it is possible that the years of anxiety about his health persuaded everyone, himself included, that he would always be 'delicate'; and his medical history may even have put paid to his plans to enter the diplomatic service.

After studying hard at home, he finally entered Balliol College, Oxford, in 1903, and graduated in 1906 with a first-class in finals—the first modern-language candidate to offer Russian. This was followed by a Leipzig doctorate under Leskien in 1910, and in the same year he was appointed Reader in Russian in the University of Oxford.

A letter to his sister in 1905 shows the continuing closeness of their relationship:

I am as you know not effusive of words, so I can never say how happy I am when I am with you. . . . Surely you need never repent saying anything to me whatever it be, for what is the good of being brother and sister if we cannot always say what we think and feel. I think that when we both feel as we do, the sense of secure love of which you write, nothing more, not even [its] expression, is needed.

And, in 1913, answering a letter in which she sent him greetings on his thirtieth birthday, he wrote: 'I really have "nothing whatever to grumble at", and yet the world is not at all "dull and flat" . . . you must now believe me when I say I have *now got all I want* and am perfectly happy.'

This account does not, of course, attempt to assess Nevill Forbes's contribution to Slavonic studies;[6] nor is it a complete life-story, for in a sense his life was not 'completed'; nor can I attempt to assess the effects that his unusual upbringing had on the development of his psyche—though it must have added to the pressures on a highly sensitive personality with a tendency to hypochondria. We, his four nieces, knew him only as our uncle, and as such he was a great success. When we returned from Palestine in 1923 we had the chance to get to know him a little, and we enjoyed him. We appreciated his generosity while laughing at his 'fussiness'. Whenever he arrived on a visit he would ask, before kissing us, if we had colds, then present each of us with a crisp new £1 note—a big present for little girls in the 1920s. He would play the piano endlessly for us, repeating our favourites again and again. I never remember his playing from music, and the repertoire of largely French and Russian works, as well as Chopin and Liszt, that he knew by heart must have been enormous. My one regret is (as so often happens in life) that only too late did I think of the questions to which I would so much like to have had answers. A letter from my mother to my father while she was on a visit to Oxford in 1926 is perceptive. She wrote:

This place always tends to Lotus-eating . . . it is still all so beautiful here. . . . Nevill's little garden is crammed with blossom and the river full and rushing past behind the tulips and the flowering chestnut trees make it Venetian in feeling . . . the two doggoes are great fun and Nevill so happy in his lot and content, that one forgets to lament his ineffectualness, or rather, *not* 'sich geltend machen', for I don't think he does really put his talent enough out to interest. But it is evident that wherever he goes he is liked and welcomed, and I daresay that is better than a title or the headship of a college—cosmically better, I mean.

And yet, less than three years later, it was apparently no longer satisfying enough. His suicide just before his forty-sixth birthday shook the calm of my childhood, for it was the first time that I saw my mother cry.[7]

---

[6] Obituaries appeared in *The Times* (11 February 1929, p. 14; 12 February, p. 9; 20 February, p. 19), and in the *Slavonic and East European Review*, vii (1928–9), 699–702.

[7] His death occurred on 9 February and the inquest is reported in *The Times* of 12 February, p. 9; from its findings it is clear that Nevill was a sick man at the time of his death and that he had been suffering from fits of depression.

The Origins of Socialist Realism in Soviet Visual Art

By JANA HOWLETT

In September 1973 an article entitled 'Socialist Realism in the light of international debate', by A. Ovcharenko, appeared in the journal *Molodaya gvardiya*. The article contained an account of the birth of the term 'Socialist Realism', which, according to Ovcharenko, was first formulated in late April 1932 at a meeting between the Central Committee of the Communist Party of the USSR and its newly-created Organizing Committee for the Restructuring of Artistic Organizations (chairman: I. M. Gronsky). During discussion of the 'basic creative method of Soviet society' Stalin asked Gronsky to propose a definition. Gronsky's answer was 'Communist Realism'. But Stalin pointed out that in view of the stage of development which Soviet society had then reached this term would not be accurate, and 'Socialist Realism' was adopted instead.

This meeting took place in the closing phase of a *literary* debate which ended in the dissolution of the numerous literary organizations still existing in that year, and in the formation of the Union of Writers. The term 'Socialist Realism' as conceived in 1932 originated, therefore, with reference to literature, and defined method rather than style—a distinction frequently stressed by later theorists of Soviet art. Yet in painting and visual art generally it has come to be associated with a specific stylistic treatment of a now familiar range of subject-matter, whose best-known exponents, such as Gerasimov and Brodsky, have earned for it the ironic definition current in Eastern Europe: 'Socialist Realism is a method of portraying our leaders in a way they will understand'.

By 1934 Socialist Realism had gained so strong an official position that any style or subject in visual art that could not be accommodated under its umbrella was dismissed as 'formalist' or 'decadent'. Indeed, for many years its power as a school of painting was so dominant that it became almost impossible to believe in the existence of such an episode as the 'Great Experiment'—the name given by Camilla Gray to the wide variety of trends that vied for pre-eminence in Russian art between 1863 and 1922.[1]

This article is an attempt to provide some answers to the question of how this term, intended originally to define and prescribe literary method, has come to signify a style in visual art that has all but obliterated the achievement of several generations of artists—artists, moreover, who continued to exercise an influence on Western art long after their activities in Russia had ceased. These answers must be sought both in Russian art before and immediately after the Revolution and in the arts policy of the young Soviet state.

[1] C. Gray, *The Great Experiment: Russian Art, 1863–1922* (1962).

In 1910 Alexander Benois wrote:

A bird's-eye view of the Russian art scene might present the following picture: to the right lie the withered, desiccated and dusty 'old schools'; in the centre blooms the Union of Artists and groups associated with it; to the left the shoots of young plants can only just be seen. . . . Beneath the wilting shadows which lie across the unswept paths of the official garden one or two people are taking a stroll and trying to look as if they are enjoying themselves. The central, cool and blossoming garden is more populous, but everyone there is trying to break, pluck or trample on something. As for the third garden, this is empty of all save the gardeners—outsiders only look in for a laugh. . . .[2]

The dusty official garden represented the *Peredvizhniki*—the Union of Travelling Art Exhibitions, formed in the 1860s in reaction against the detached academic classicism of the St. Petersburg Academy. The *Peredvizhniki* were the first painters in Russia to pose the question of social responsibility in art and of art as social propaganda; however, by the 1890s their 'literary method' and categorical pronouncements (such as Chistyakov's 'in a serious painting everything must be subordinated to the meaning'[3]) had alienated many of their younger disciples, who formed the second generation of *Peredvizhniki*—painters of tranquil, serene landscapes and portraits.

These were the predecessors of the blossoming garden—Benois's own *Mir iskusstva* and the *Soyuz russkich khudozhnikov*[4], which at various times included Bakst, Kuznetsov, the Symbolists Čiurlionis, Roerich (Rerikh), Borisov-Musatov, the Milyuti brothers and many more. In their reaction to the *Peredvizhniki*, these artists not only opposed the notion of art as social propaganda—they also advocated close study of all artistic models, from Eastern and Western classical art and Russian and Byzantine iconography to the contemporary art of Western Europe.

The exhibitions mounted by the members of this 'blossoming garden' were among the most outstanding contributions to the development of Russian art. They included those organized by the journal *Zolotoe runo* in 1908 and 1909, which brought work of the French symbolists and impressionists to Russia, and the 1922 St. Petersburg exhibition, '100 Years of French Painting', which introduced the Russian public to some of the most important painters, from the period of the French Revolution to Cézanne and the post-impressionists. But *Mir iskusstva* and its associated groups did more than bring Western art to Russia: they—and especially Benois and Diaghilev—encouraged fruitful cross-fertilization by showing examples of contemporary Russian art side by side with those of the West, and by taking exhibitions of Russian artists to

[2] A. Benois, 'Itogi', *Rech'*, 26 March 1910.

[3] AN SSSR, *Istoriya russkogo iskusstva*, ii (M., 1960), 100.

[4] Groups such as the *Peredvizhniki* and *Mir iskusstva* had an artistic programme, but this does not mean that artists exhibiting with them shared this programme. Several artists exhibited with more than one society, not infrequently with societies of seemingly opposing views. Cf. S. Gorodetsky's statement: 'Scratch anyone from the *Soyuz russkikh khudozhnikov* and you'll find a *Peredvizhnik*', in *Zolotoe runo*, 1909 no. 11/12, p. 93.

France and Germany. Many 'young shoots', such as Kandinsky and Petrov-Vodkin, were later to acknowledge their debt to *Mir iskusstva*.

The early years of the twentieth century were a period of considerable mobility when many Russian artists, like their Western colleagues, were drawn to the various European capitals. A vivid picture of the artistic society of Europe has been given by Hans Richter,[5] who describes how, in the years leading up to the First World War, a sort of 'café clique' formed itself in every major city. All schools of thought would here contend and coalesce, sharing the one common conviction that the old world was doomed and that its last years should best be spent in learning all there was to know about art, before it expired together with the bourgeoisie to whom it belonged. The art produced in this atmosphere may be seen as branching into two main streams. The one, analytical and rational, emerged as Cubism, its offshoot Orphism, and the Italian Futurist movement. The other stream, subjective, tending toward the irrational, emphasized the music of colour and the role of the subconscious and gave birth to Fauvism, German and Scandinavian Expressionism, Dada and irrational abstract art.

In 1909 the 'young shoots' appeared to be more receptive to the latter influence: at the third *Zolotoe runo* exhibition, symbolist paintings of Petrov-Vodkin were hung alongside the works of David Burlyuk and Pavel Kuznetsov (both then under the sway of Fauvism), while Larionov and Goncharova showed their 'Primitivist' pictures. The *doyen* of the *Peredvizhniki*, Repin, reacted to this exhibition in a manner remarkably reminiscent of later pronouncements by the guardians of Socialist Realism: '. . . a complete hell of cynicism and Western trash'.[6]

A year or two later, however, the 'rational stream' had become dominant among the younger generation—as exemplified in Malevich's experiments in the division of space by colour, plane and volume in the 1910–13 series of 'peasant' paintings (*Gathering the Harvest, Woman with Buckets, Head of a Peasant Girl*), and in the Orphist and Rayonist paintings of Larionov and Goncharova, dating from 1911 onward. But perhaps the clearest indication of this parallel development of 'rational' art in Russia and the West is to be seen in the similar, yet varying, analyses of motion as painted by Duchamp (*Nude descending a staircase, No. 2*, 1912), Feininger (*Cyclists*, 1912), Goncharova (*Cyclists*, 1912–13), Malevich (*The Knife-Grinder*, 1912), and in the relation between material and subject as dissected in works by Braque, Picasso, Malevich, Udal'tsova, Popova and Tatlin that were executed shortly before the war.

Just as the outbreak of war in 1914 signalized for many the death of the old society, so for many it was also a time of decision: conscription and the closing of the frontiers meant that a choice had to be made between Russia and exile, the army and pacifism. Some, Like Larionov and Goncharova, left Russia, while others, like Chagall and Kandinsky, decided to return. Some, like Filonov and Petrov-Vodkin, felt it their duty to fight, while Mayakovsky, Tatlin and others devised *Spektakli* in Petrograd and Moscow, similar to those of the Dadaists in Zürich.

[5] H. Richter, *Dada* (1962).
[6] *Birzhevye vedomosti*, 20 May 1910.

But it was not only in the impulse to *épater les bourgeois*, nor in the realization that they were in fact entertaining the bourgeoisie rather than shocking
them, that the now isolated Russian *avant-garde* came close to the *avant-garde*
of Europe. The sense of futility and uncertainty that pervades the work of
artists such as Malevich (e.g. *An Englishman in Moscow*, 1915) and Filonov
was shared by many Europeans, among them the German George Grosz and
the Rumanian–Swiss Marcel Janco.

For the young artists not actually on military service the years from 1915
to 1917 could be described as a period of consolidation and decision. In the
activities of those extremists who came to be known as the 'Left', the word
'last' figures frequently: in 1915 Malevich exhibited his *Last Suprematist
Painting*, and together with Klyun, Tatlin and Puni, organized '0,10—the
Last Futurist Exhibition'. This intimation of finality so rapidly attained by
the 'young shoots' of 1910 was to have a very potent effect on the development
of art after the Revolution. Undoubtedly, by 1917 the garden was fully
grown and had no further need of cultivation.

That this was the only major alteration in the picture as presented by
Benois seven years earlier can be seen from a list of some of the principal
exhibitions held in Moscow and Petrograd on the eve of the Bolshevik
Revolution. The Futurists (by then a collective term which, like 'Leftists',
was used to describe the extreme *avant-garde*) presented 'The Shop' in Moscow; the fourth exhibition of the *Bubnovyi valet* group (founded in 1911 and
uniting such artists as Fal'k, Yakulov and Konchalovsky, who were sometimes
known as the 'Russian Cézannistes') showed their work in both capitals; so
did the *Peredvizhniki*, who opened their 44th exhibition on 20 December 1916.
This record makes it clear that the *avant-garde*, active as it was, was neither
the only, nor the dominant, force in Russian art prior to the Revolution.

From the manifestos and other publications of the major artistic groupings
at this time, it is also clear that although most artists were no doubt acutely
aware of art as a social or anti-social force, they avoided commitment to any
party-political line. This was particularly evident at the time of the Bolshevik
uprising in the artists' attitude toward the new government and toward the
Revolution itself. Perhaps the most telling expression of the mixed feelings
of many regarding this momentous event occurs in a letter by N. N. Kupreyanov, whose work and artistic sympathies place him among the moderate
'Leftists'.[7] He wrote to his wife in October 1917:

. . . I am sitting in the dining-room, alone, under a terrible light from a
lamp with no shade, and I can't work. Not because of the lamp, but because
of the heavy and oppressive mood I'm in. I feel depressed, attacked by a sort
of spiritual weakness. It seems to me now that if we should have to face
danger I will have neither courage nor strength. I can't think why, for I
have been so calm all this time, thinking of nothing except 'The Cart-horse'
[an engraving that Kupreyanov was engaged on at the time] . . .
A battleship[8] is lying in the Neva opposite the Admiralty. I have just
passed it—all was darkness and gloom. Murky whiteness surrounded its
lights. The silhouette of the ship was beautiful and sombre. . . .

[7] N. S. Iznar and M. Z. Kholodovskaya, *N.N. Kupreyanov* (M., 1973).
[8] The *Avrora*, which had given the signal for the storming of the Winter Palace in October 1917.

I remember the night I was on observation duty under Tarnopol'—the shells, probably all from one gun, fell nearer and nearer, at regular intervals, and then somehow passed us by. I felt great danger, and yet no fear, I felt the absolute inevitablity of that which had to happen. . . . Today there is no such certainty.[9]

But at first 'certainty' did not seem especially to be called for—and few artists, even among the 'Leftists', could be said to have 'leapt to the cause of the Revolution'.[10] Their response was confined to an aesthetic curiosity: most of them waited to see what would happen. Artists felt the need to define their position only as it began to dawn on them that, with the state as sole patron of the arts, their attitude to the new government involved matters of patronage as well as of politics.

In considering the relationship between the artists and their new patron it is first of all necessary to look at certain aspects of Bolshevik theory worked out before the Revolution—aspects which had a particular bearing on this question.

The *Vpered* group, headed by Bogdanov and Gor'ky, were among the few Bolshevik theoreticians to concern themselves with art and the problem of relations between the artist and the state. Their discussions, however, were occupied principally with literature, since they considered the printed word to be the basic vehicle of polemic and thus its status in relation to the state and censorship to be in most urgent need of definition. The group's insistence on the right of cultural organizations to be independent of the Party caused a serious rift among the Bolsheviks. Although *Vpered* and Lenin had become reconciled by 1915, the argument about cultural autonomy remained unresolved until after the Revolution.

As for visual art, it can definitely be said that at the time there existed no clear Party 'line'—there were merely certain 'tastes' among the leadership, which occasionally found expression in the columns of *Pravda*. Typical of this was an article published in 1914, which stated: 'The decadents are attacking the renewal of realism because they feel that realism expresses the power of the workers' movement'.[11] The working out of a 'line' was left almost entirely in the hands of A. V. Lunacharsky, whose appointment as People's Commissar for Education on 26 October 1917, a few days after the Bolsheviks came to power, made him responsible for all matters connected with the arts.

However suitable the choice of Lunacharsky may have been, his appointment to this post was an indication of the secondary importance attached by the Party to education and the arts at this stage. Moreover, owing to his *Vpered* associations Lunacharsky was never really regarded by Lenin as politically trustworthy, and this distrust made the Commissar's position peculiarly difficult: he found himself confronted with the open hostility of those he was supposed to administer, with little financial or organizational support from the new government. As head of an institution which, by the end of 1918, had nearly 50 departments and a staff of over 3,000 (ten times that of the old

[9] Iznar, *Kupreyanov* (n. 7), 112.
[10] Gray, op. cit. (n. 1), 219.
[11] *Dooktyabr'skaya 'Pravda' ob iskusstve i literature* (M., 1937), 17.

Ministry of Education), Lunacharsky's responsibilities ranged from nursery-schools to the management of theatres and publishing houses. His first task was to find competent help in running the Commissariat—and, as Sheila Fitzpatrick points out in her study of this institution,[12] Party members were notoriously unwilling to work for the Commissariat for Education (*Narkompros*). Lunacharsky was obliged to seek assistance elsewhere.

Finding a suitable individual to lead the work of *IZO Narkompros* (*Izobrazitel'nyi otdel Narodnogo komissariata prosveshcheniya*) proved no easy matter, for the numerous artistic groups in Moscow and Petrograd seemed, for once, to be united—in their distrust of Lunacharsky. Some of the most virulent attacks upon the Commissariat were made by 'Leftists' such as Al'tman and Punin; the common ground of all such opposition was the fear that the government would deprive artistic organizations of their autonomy.

That Lunacharsky himself was well aware of this fear is clear from a speech he gave on the occasion of the dissolution of the Academy of Arts, in April 1918. In outlining *Narkompros* policy for the arts, he made three main points:

1. Art was separate from the state;
2. *Narkompros* was concerned with art only in its educational aspects;
3. No artistic group would be singled out for state support.

This speech, despite the occasion on which it was made, marked a turning point in relations between *Narkompros* and the artistic community; it is significant that one of the first artists to join the Commissariat was Benois. He accepted responsibility for the Committee for the Protection of Historic and Artistic Monuments (a body he had helped to found during the war years), and became Director of the Hermitage Museum. Benois's activities in the *Mir iskusstva* and the *Soyuz russkikh khudozhnikov*, and his exceptionally clear art criticism, had won him the respect of almost everyone in the artistic community—and he was soon joined at *Narkompros* by several artists of the 'Centre' and the 'Left', who took over administration and teaching in the various organizations formed to replace the Academy of Arts in Petrograd and the Institute of Painting, Sculpture, and Architecture in Moscow. The most notable of these individuals were: Petrov-Vodkin (Committee for the Re-organization of the Academy), Lentulov (Svomas—*Svobodnye masterskie*—in Moscow), Shterenberg and Al'tman (Petrograd IZO), and Tatlin (Moscow IZO).

The brief honeymoon that followed, when it seemed as if artists of every faction were willing to sink their differences and co-operate with the government, was centred around the celebration of the first anniversary of the Bolshevik Revolution—the plan for which was drawn up by Lenin personally. Inspired apparently by the *Civitas Solis* of Campanella, it envisaged the ceremonial destruction of tsarist monuments and the inauguration of monuments expressing the spirit of the new state, to the accompaniment of an intensive propaganda campaign in the press and in all public places.

[12] S. Fitzpatrick, *The Commissariat of Enlightenment: Soviet Organisation of the Arts under Lunacharsky, October 1917–1921* (Cambridge, 1970).

Execution of the plan was entrusted to Lunacharsky, who had to undertake this daunting task on a low budget and with a chaotic administration.

All was to be ready by 1 May 1918, but there were various delays and on 12 May Lenin wrote a furious letter to the Moscow Soviet, castigating it for its inefficiency and ending: 'Forgive this open expression of my opinion and accept my communist greetings, which I send in the hope that you will end up in prison for your lack of action. Yours indignantly, Lenin'.[13]

The sculptors were assigned the most difficult part of the programme. In Moscow alone they were expected to submit projects for sixty-seven monuments not less than twelve feet in height, to be executed in 'temporary material'. Each successful entry was to receive a prize of 7,000 roubles, which had to cover the cost of a stone plinth as well as of the work itself (that same year, a prize of 1,000,000 roubles was offered for a 'social novel'). Ten weeks was the time-limit set for this work, so it is hardly surprising that by 7 November only thirty-one pieces of sculpture were ready.

The painters did rather better. In spite of considerable difficulties, both Moscow and Petrograd were draped with posters and colourful designs in time for the celebrations on 1 May and 7 November. The cities had been divided into sections, each to be decorated by an artist or group of artists, and in his memoirs of this occasion I. Zakharov writes: 'I was commissioned to decorate Zubov Square [in Moscow]. I had no experience in such matters. We were given excellent white linen and red cloth. The boulevard entrance was adorned with heavy, awkward arches made of logs which we hung with slogans and cloth. . . . We had to do all the work at the offices of the district committee. For security reasons a guard was assigned to us, because the intelligentsia were then not particularly trusted. . . .'[14]

We do not know of all the artists who carried out the decoration of Moscow, but we have a list for Petrograd[15] in which we find names from among all the major art groupings. Brodsky, Savitsky and the *Obshchestvo imeni A. Kuindzhi* represented those associated with the *Peredvizhniki*; the 'Centre' contributed designs by Dobuzhinsky, Petrov-Vodkin, Kustodiev and others; among the 'Leftists' were members of the 'Proletkul't' group, as well as Lebedev, Al'tman, Shterenberg and Baranoff-Rossiné. The 'Left', however, did not play the most important role: the greatest contribution came from the 'Centre', and contemporary photographs of such sites as Theatre Square suggest that their romantic symbolism was especially well suited to the occasion.

This short-lived collaboration was over by 1919, by which time the polarization of the art groups was such as to preclude any further possibilities of joint action. That this was in no way due to government interference is clear from the very general character of the only major statement on the arts issued by the Party in that year: 'There is no branch of science or the arts which is not connected with the great ideas of communism'.[16] At the same

[13] *Leninskii sbornik*, xxi, 215.

[14] A. S. Galushkina, *et al.*, *Agitatsionno-massovoe iskusstvo pervykh let Oktyabrya* (M., 1971), 35.

[15] Ibid. 50.

[16] *KPSS v rezolyutsiyakh i resheniyakh s"ezdov konferentsii i plenumov Tsentral'nogo komiteta*, pt. 1 (1954), 64.

time Lunacharsky, writing in the *Narkompros* journal *Iskusstvo kommuny*, was careful to stress that, while welcoming the co-operation of the 'Leftists', the government did not consider them the sole representatives of Soviet art.

The 'Leftists' themselves were increasingly of another opinion. In January 1919 an article by B. Kushner stated: 'Revolutionary opposition has risen from the very depths of bourgeois culture. The name of this opposition is futurism. . . . We must make the incredible leap straight to socialism'.[17] In order to make this leap it was necessary, according to Kushner, for artists to produce 'articles of daily use' and not just 'pretty pictures'. But Lunacharsky's attitude to 'pretty pictures' was rather different: in 1919, as one of a jury which included Blok, Gor'ky and Andreeva, he awarded first prize to I. I. Brodsky for a painting entitled *Lenin and the Demonstration*.

Brodsky, who had been a pupil of the great *Peredvizhnik* Repin, was an accomplished painter whose work was much admired by Gor'ky in 1910, when the artist stayed with him on Capri and painted his portrait. Before the Revolution, which was to make Lenin the central subject of his work (1924: *Lenin against the background of a demonstration*; 1925: *Lenin against the background of Smol'ny*; 1927: *Lenin against the background of Volkhovstroi*, etc.), Brodsky had already established his reputation with paintings such as *The Red Funeral* (1906), *The Demonstration of the Tsar's Faithful Servants in Gratitude for the Saving of their Fatherland* (1914), and with portraits of Kerensky and other leaders of the Provisional Government (1917).

This painter, and others like him, carried on with their work and received commissions and prizes, while it became increasingly obvious that the artists of the 'Left' were spending their time in teaching and theorizing about the relation of art to society. 'Leftists' did indeed participate in a number of exhibitions in the early years of the Revolution, but most of the work they showed was retrospective. And in spite of the proliferation of factions and the vigorous controversies between such groups as Filonov's Expressionist-Analysts, Malevich's Suprematists, Tatlin's Constructivists and Rodchenko's Productionists—arguments giving an impression of strength and vitality—the artists of 'Leftist' persuasion had rendered themselves vulnerable by their theories and by their political attitudes. Many of them had reached the conclusion that easel-painting was dead because it was the art of bourgeois society: they considered that it was their task to create a new art for an entirely new, classless society. Some, like Naum Gabo and Archipenko, maintained that this new art was to be found in abstraction which, they felt, could hold no class associations since it had no known associations at all. Others believed the answer to lie in production art—art objects for daily use. But whatever their ideas, the artists of the 'Left' looked for approval to the new society for which they were working. And this approval was not forthcoming—for workers' juries, factory visits and attempts at art education of the masses were making it clear that Lunacharsky was correct in claiming that the workers wanted pictures rather than experiments.[18]

As a result, the 'Leftists' retreated more and more into theory, increasing

[17] *Iskusstvo kommuny*, 26 Jan. 1919.
[18] A. V. Lunacharsky, 'Iskusstvo i rabochii klass', *Chetyre goda AKhRR* (M., 1926), 19.

their isolation from the society with which they so wished to be identified. This very isolation, perhaps, prevented them from realizing that, by claiming their own art to be more politically correct than that of any other group, they laid themselves open to attack on political grounds.

The first such attack came soon after a speech made by Tatlin at the VIIIth Congress of the Soviets in 1921, in which he declared: 'What happened from the social point of view in 1917 had been recognized in our work as visual artists in 1914. . . .'[19] Characteristically, the attack did not emanate from the Party but from a group of artists associated with the *Peredvizhniki*—in an article signed by Brodsky and entitled 'On the breakdown of artistic life and urgent measures for its restoration'.[20] This article appealed directly to Lenin for help against *Narkompros*, which, it was claimed, favoured the destructive tendencies of the 'Leftists'.

Lunacharsky found it increasingly difficult to defend the 'Leftists', especially since he had more sympathy for their willingness to help than for their artistic aims. And these were deeply distrusted by the Bolshevik leadership—as is evident from a speech by Lenin on the occasion of the dissolution of Proletkul't[21] in 1920: '. . . Proletkul't attracted socially alien elements . . . futurists, decadents, defenders of idealistic philosophy, which is an enemy of Marxism'.[22] These words referred primarily to writers, but by implication 'futurist' artists were among those condemned.

Meanwhile, the artists of the 'Centre' and the *Peredvizhniki* went from strength to strength. In 1920 Brodsky was asked to form a small group to make portraits of delegates to the Second Congress of the Communist International. This commission, which took four years to complete, was carried out by members of the *Peredvizhniki* and the *Obshchestvo imeni A. Kuindzhi* and artists from 'Centre' organizations such as the *Soyuz russkikh khudozhnikov*. Whatever their stylistic differences, the *Soyuz russkikh khudozhnikov* and the *Peredvizhniki* artists found it quite possible to collaborate.

Between 1921 and 1932 numerous decrees were issued regarding the arts (*iskusstvo*), but these were concerned almost exclusively with the press. And the attitude of the Party leadership which saw the visual arts as a rather ineffectual appendage to literature had the effect, for some time, of protecting the artists from political pressure. But notwithstanding statements such as that made by Krupskaya about one of Brodsky's portraits of Lenin ('Photographs are better. They always show the truth.'[23]), the increase in government patronage for artists of *Peredvizhniki* sympathies demonstrated where the preferences of the leadership lay.

This confidence in the *Peredvizhniki* was not misplaced. In 1922 the group mounted its 47th exhibition in Moscow and published a statement of its aims:

---

[19] Quoted in J. E. Bowlt, 'Russian Art in the Nineteen Twenties', *Soviet Studies*, xxii, 576.

[20] Quoted in I. A. Brodsky, *Isaak Izrailevich Brodsky* (M., 1973), 198.

[21] Proletkul't was part of *Narkompros* and was originally entrusted with 'proletarian culture', i.e. educational measures among the workers. Led by Bogdanov, Proletkul't tried to take over all the functions of *Narkompros* until Lunacharsky was forced to appeal for help to the Central Committee and Proletkul't was dissolved.

[22] *Bor'ba za realizm v izobrazitel'nom iskusstve 20-kh godov* (M., 1962), 63–5.

[23] Quoted in Brodsky, op. cit. (n. 20), 401.

'We want to capture the life of contemporary Russia through the documentary accuracy of our genre-, portrait-, and landscape-painting, and to show the working life of all its nationalities.'[24] In the same year AKhRR (*Assotsiatsiya khudozhnikov revolyutsionnoi Rossii*) was founded, with a manifesto proclaiming ideas very similar to those of the *Peredvizhniki* quoted above: 'Our civic duty to humanity is to provide an artistic-documentary record of the greatest moment of history—its revolutionary outburst'.[25]

By now the 'Left' was in an extremely weak position, several of its most prominent members, including Kandinsky, Lissitsky, Gabo and Pevsner, having left Russia for the West, driven out by petty internal squabbles and by the desperate economic situation in which they found themselves. In 1921 the Productionists Rodchanko, Exter and Popova declared that 'easel-painting is extinct and our activity as mere painters useless'—and turned to industrial and book design and the cinema. And when, in 1925, a group of VKhuTEMAS (*Vysshie khudozhestvenno-tekhnicheskie masterskie*) students led by Pimenov and Deineka formed OST (*Obshchestvo stankovistov*), in protest against the dictatorial experimentalism of their teachers, the 'Left' had indeed lost almost all support.

In the years leading up to the dissolution of all artistic organizations and the inception of the Union of Artists of the USSR in 1932, AKhRR became steadily more influential. By 1926 it had enrolled many prominent *Peredvizhniki* (Brodsky, Savitsky, Moravov and others), *Mir iskusstva* and *Soyuz russkikh khudozhnikov* figures (Kustodiev, Arkhipov, Yuon), and other 'Centrists' (Mashkov, Konchalovsky, Fal'k). Lunacharsky, too, had retreated completely from the principles he had enunciated in 1918. (In 1926 he declared: 'AKhRR is now the main stream of our visual art and the latest works of its artists indicate the type of art which will clearly become dominant'.[26])

It is true that, despite increased political support after 1928, the principles of AKhRR did not find easy acceptance, until the formation of the Union of artists in 1932. But with the disintegration of the 'Left' there remained no grouping strong enough to challenge this alliance of *Peredvizhniki*, *Soyuz russkikh khudozhnikov* and the *Bubnovyi valet*. However, the real strength of AKhRR may have lain in the formulation it provided for Socialist Realism in painting. Its call for 'heroic realism'[27] and portrayal of the 'life and work of the nationalities of the USSR'[28] was made almost ten years before Socialist Realism was defined as an art which is national in form and socialist in content.

The Communist Party's appreciation of the work of AKhRR and its leading personalities was shown in the support it gave the organization (after 1928, AKhR—*Assotsiatsiya khudozhnikov Rossii*) in its struggle for dominance. And one of the clearest expressions of the Party's gratitude appeared in a speech made at a meeting of the Union of Artists in 1933 by the man to

[24] Op. cit. (n. 22), 120.
[25] AKhRR declaration, in *Chetyre goda AKhRR* (n. 18), 9.
[26] *Izvestiya*, 30 May 1926.
[27] AKhRR declaration (n. 25).
[28] Title of exhibition organized by AKhRR in 1926.

whom the term 'Socialist Realism' owed its existence, I. M. Gronsky, who said: 'When we need to answer the English imperialists who are fomenting war against us by their attempts at sabotaging the building of socialism, the Party's newspaper *Pravda* publishes *The Execution of the Twenty-six Baku Commissars*, by Brodsky. . . . This is the art that is needed, it helps the struggle, the building of socialism and the defence of the Fatherland. . . . With Brodsky we will win, with the formalists we will not'.[29]

[29] Brodsky, op. cit. (n. 20), 265.

The Implications of
Richard James's *maimanto*

by MICHAEL HEANEY

l'EW words can have had more etymons proposed for them than has the word *mammoth*. At various times its origin has been sought in the Estonian word for 'mole', the Tungus for 'bear', the Arabic form of 'behemoth', the Russian name for Saint Mamas, and the Tatar for 'earth'. This last etymology has long been discredited, though it still occurs from time to time, even in Osborn's definitive work on the Proboscidea:

In allusion to the fact that the Tatars of Siberia first discovered the ivory tusks by digging in the earth, the word 'mammoth' is certainly derived from the alleged Tatar word *mamma*, signifying 'earth'. As early as 1696 this was combined with another Tatar word *kost*, signifying 'ivory', and the two words were Latinized by Ludolf as *Mammotovoi Kost*.[1]

As the Oxford English Dictionary points out, 'the alleged Tatar word *mama* "earth" (usually cited as the etymon) is not known to exist'.[2]

A more realistic suggestion comes from Räsänen, who relates the word to the Tungus *ŋāmę-ndi*, 'bear'.[3] However, there are several objections to this etymology, not least that it is unlikely that a word which must be in common use in the Tungus-speaking area should be applied to two totally different animals. There is no evidence to suggest that the concepts of 'bear' and 'mammoth' are confused or even linked in Tungus mythology.

One of the earliest references to the mammoth gives another etymology for the word which has occasionally found support elsewhere. The reference occurs in Strahlenberg's description of Siberia. It will be discussed in greater detail later, but the essence of the explanation lies in relating 'mammoth' to the Arabic *mehemot*:

. . . it doubtless has its origin from the *Hebrew* and *Arabick*; this word denoting *Behemot*, of which Job speaks . . . and which the *Arabs* pronounce *Mehemot*: but our commentators are not agreed, what kind of animal is to be understood by *Behemot* . . . and it seems the *Arabians* were not at a greater certainty. However, this is certain, that they brought this word into Greater Tartary; for the *Ostiacks* near the River *Oby*, call the *mammoth Khosar*, and the *Tartars* call it *Khir*; and though the *Arabian* name of an elephant is *Fyhl*, yet, if very large, they add the adjective *Mehemodi* to it; and these *Arabs* coming into Tartary, and finding there the relics of some monstrous great beast, not certain of what kind they might be, they called these teeth

---

[1] H. F. Osborn, *Proboscidea*, ii (New York, 1942), 1164.

[2] *OED*, s.v. *mammoth*.

[3] M. Räsänen, 'Das Wort Mammut', *Zeitschrift für slavische Philologie*, xxi (1951), 293–5.

Mehemot, which afterwards became a proper name, among the *Tartars*; and, by the *Russians*, is corruptly pronounced *Mammoth*.[4]

The most extensive discussion of the question has come from van der Meulen.[5] He examines the problem in great detail, and comes to two main conclusions. The first is that the form current in most Western European languages, characterized by the absence of an *n* (e.g. German *Mammut*, English *mammoth*), derives from a spelling error in what he believed to be the earliest reference to the mammoth in Western literature, namely Witsen's mention of 'Mammouttekoos' and 'Mammout'.[6] Van der Meulen claims that the *u* in these words is a misreading of *n*, and that the correct reading should be 'Mammont'. He cites similar misreadings from other places in the text. The second conclusion he draws is that the Russian form of the word is derived from Polish *mamona* 'monster' via the form *mamon*. He explains the influence of Polish by the presence of large numbers of Polish exiles in Russia after the Thirteen Years' War between Russia and Poland during the seventeenth century.

The etymologies so far cited suffer from the disadvantage that when they were proposed the earliest known reference to the mammoth was Witsen's, dating from 1692. But in 1951 J. S. G. Simmons and B. O. Unbegaun pointed out a much earlier reference to the mammoth by Richard James in 1618.[7] The work at that time existed only in manuscript (Oxf. Bodl. MS James 43*) but has since been published by Larin.[8] In 1954 V. Kiparsky suggested that James's version of the word, *maimanto*, should be read as *mammanto* (a suggestion not supported by the manuscript), and derived the word from the Yurak Samoyed *jēaŋ ŋammurɔ̄tpȝ̂* 'earth eater', basing his argument largely on the geminate -*mm*-. Vasmer notes James's form, but refrains from coming to a firm decision on the etymology of the word.[9] This is a pity, as both the form of the word and the date of its occurrence are very significant.

James's *Dictionariolum Russico-Anglicum* was compiled in 1618–19. On page 62 of the manuscript (page 181 of Larin's edition) occur the following words:

slone, an elephant
maimanto, as they say a sea elephant, which is never seene, but according to the Samyites he workes himselfe under grownde and so they find his teeth or hornes or bones in Pechore and Nova Zemla, of which they make table men in Russia.

[4] P. von Strahlenberg, *An Historico–Geographical Description of the North and Eastern Parts of Europe and Asia* (1748), 403. I have unfortunately not been able to consult the original German text, published in Stockholm, 1730.

[5] R. van der Meulen, 'De naam van den mammouth', *Mededeelingen, Koninklijke Akademie van wetenschappen te Amsterdam, Afdeeling letterkunde, Deel 63, Serie A*, no. 12 (1927), 349–403.

[6] N. Witsen, *Noord en Oost Tartarye*, pt. 2 (Amsterdam, 1692), 472.

[7] J. S. G. Simmons and B. O. Unbegaun, 'Slavonic Manuscript Vocabularies in the Bodleian Library', *Oxford Slavonic Papers*, ii (1951), 123–5. This appeared at the same time as Räsänen's article (n. 3), so Räsänen was unable to use the information in his article. Consequently Unbegaun gave further notice of *maimanto* in 'Zum russischen Namen des Mammuts', *Zeitschrift für slavische Philologie*, xxii (1954), 150–1.

[8] B. A. Larin, *Russko-angliiskii slovar'-dnevnik Richarda Dzheimsa* (L., 1959).

[9] V. Kiparsky, 'Das Mammut', *Zeitschrift für slavische Philologie*, xxvi (1958), 296–300; M. Vasmer, *Russisches etymologisches Wörterbuch*, ii (Heidelberg, 1955), 93–4.

This could perhaps be taken to refer to the walrus, but on page 18a of the manuscript (Larin, p. 93) we find:

mors, a sea horse of whose teeth Mr John Nash had 4 which weied each 8 pɣndes quos estimavit pret(io) 40 librarum.

James's *maimanto* would seem to confirm van der Meulen's contention that the form in *n* is the earlier form. However, it also casts serious doubt on his explanation of the derivation of the word, as it puts the appearance of the word in the Russian language back to a date before there were appreciable numbers of Polish exiles in Siberia. It also has implications for the other proposed etymologies of the word.

Maimanto has the digraph *ai* in the first syllable. Larin reads this as the diphthong [aj],[10] but the vowel [e] seems more likely. The 96 instances of -*ai*- in James's work (exluding *maimanto* itself) can be grouped as follows: 38 represent [aC′], mainly in the infinitive, e.g. *letait, gulait*; 23 represent not [aj] before a consonant, but [aj] before a vowel, e.g. *zaietz, kaiuk*. Of these, in 11 cases the following vowel is represented in the text, as in the examples given; in 12 cases the second vowel (usually [e] or [i]) is not written, as in *xozain, pochevait*. In another 22 cases *ai* occurs in final position, mostly in imperatives (*dai, prevalivai*). In three cases *ai* represents [ajC′], as in *pobyvait* (2nd pl. imperative). Only in four cases does medial *ai* represent [aj]: *gaitan, babaika, zaixa* and *daiti*. In six cases, however, the vowel represented would appear to be [e]: *baizzin* (безим), *klaie* (клей), *béllaina* (бéлена), *nelzai* (нельзé), *podimait* (подымет), and possibly *govorait* (говореть?).

The interpretation of *mai*- as [me] gains support from Strahlenberg's reference to the mammoth. His theory on the etymology of the word has been quoted above. He justifies his theory as follows:

. . . the Russian mammoth certainly came from the word *Behemot*, in which opinion I am confirmed by the testimony of an ancient Russian priest, *Gregory* by name, father-confessor to Princess Sophia, who was many years an exile in *Siberia*, from whom I was told, that formerly the name for these bones, in *Siberia*, was not *Mammoth*, but *Memoth*, and that the *Russian* dialect had made the alteration.[11]

Two independent sources, therefore, indicate that the initial syllable could be [me], and that the change [me] > [ma] has taken place. Strahlenberg's explanation also challenges van der Meulen's account of the origin of the form of the word without *n*, as he explicitly states his knowledge of the word is first-hand, not derived from Witsen. (The English translator has perhaps anglicized the word, but there is no trace of an *n*; Strahlenberg's section on the mammoth is headed 'Mamatowa-Kost'). Ludolf's reference to the mammoth,[12] which van der Meulen also traces back to Witsen, again has indications of an independent origin. While Witsen has *Mammoutte*-, Ludolf has *Mammotovoi*, which both gives a Russian ending and changes the vowel of the second syllable. The second syllable could therefore be [at], [ot]

[10] Larin, op. cit. (n. 8), 81.
[11] Strahlenberg, loc. cit. (n. 4).
[12] H. W. Ludolf, *Grammatica Russica* (Oxford, 1696; facsimile ed., Oxford, 1959)92.

or [ut]—i.e. probably a back rounded vowel—if the form without the nasal is accepted; or [ant], [ont] if the form with the nasal is accepted. A rather later reference, by Bell, drops the -*t* and has *mammon*.[13]

At this point a brief excursus on the distribution of the mammoth and of mammoth bones may be in order. The remains of various species of mammoth have been discovered over a wide area of the world. When such remains were occasionally brought to light in Europe before the nineteenth century they were usually held to be 'giants' bones'. But in the Eurasian tundra the bones are found in great quantities; natural landslips often reveal them. They were found in the past in sufficient quantities to sustain a trade in mammoth-ivory from Siberia to China and Arabia. The geographical limit of these bones in the west is formed by the River Pechora—in European, not Asiatic Russia. Mammoth bones, therefore, are fairly widespread. The same cannot be said of mammoth carcasses. The mammoth is one of the very few extinct animals which have been found with the soft tissue more or less intact. Tolmachoff[14] records a total of 39 known finds, and since his time another half dozen have been recorded. Of the 39, the majority are in Eastern Siberia, around the rivers Indigirka and Kolyma. Only three are west of the River Enisei, namely the finds by Trofimov and Schmidt in 1839 and 1864 respectively, and the very first discovery of all, recorded by Ides in 1704.[15] The exact location of this first find is unknown, and it too may have been east of the Enisei.

Even when the carcass is preserved, it need not be preserved in a recognizable state. Tolmachoff includes in his list mammoths of which only a few scraps of flesh were preserved on an otherwise bare skeleton. One of the few carcasses of the woolly rhinoceros to have been found was initially reported as a mammoth carcass, though it perforce must have lacked trunk and tusks. In Siberia west of the Enisei it is doubtful whether the native peoples had any true conception of the mammoth at all. Karjalainen gives several names for the mammoth, such as Ostyak *jəŋk-ves*, 'Wasser-ves', *ves-īkə* 'ves-Alter', and concludes: 'Aus den Erklärungen der Leute zu schliessen, wird jedoch das Mammut seinem Aussehen nach garnicht als einheitliche Tierart aufgefasst, sondern mit diesem Namen werden verschiedene Arten bezeichnet'.[16] Laufer also gives details of Ostyak misconceptions about the mammoth:

They are also fond of residing in the depth of streams and lakes, and their presence is announced by the agitation of the water and whirlpools. . . . Other animals when old may undergo a metamorphosis into mammoths; elks and reindeer, even bears, may change their status for a life in the depth of the water: when mammoth horns will grow on them. Old pikes are said sometimes to choose the deepest spots of lakes where moss will grow on their heads and horns on their front, when it is concluded that old pikes are

[13] J. Bell, *Travels from St. Petersburg in Russia to Diverse Parts of Asia*, ii (Glasgow, 1763), 148.

[14] I. P. Tolmachoff, 'The Carcasses of the Mammoth and Rhinoceros found in the Frozen Ground of Siberia', *Transactions of the American Philosophical Society*, N.S., xxiii, pt. 1 (1929).

[15] E. Y. Ides, *Driejaarige reize naar China, te lande gedaan door den Moscovischen afgezant E. Ysbrand Ides* (Amsterdam, 1704), ch. 6.

[16] K. F. Karjalainen, *Die Religion der Jugra-Völker*, iii (FF Communications, 63) (Helsinki, 1927), 29–30.

gradually transformed into mammoths. In this form they are called pike-mammoth.[17]

If, when mammoth bones were found by Ostyaks in West Siberia, they were sometimes attributed to the *ves*, it is no more significant than the attribution of similar finds in Western Europe to giants, and does not mean that *ves* was the word for 'mammoth' as we understand it. In Western Siberia at least, the identification of *ves* with the mammoth as an actual beast is very probably a result of Russian influence—as Ides writes, 'd'oude Siberische Russen zeggen en gelooven, dat de Mammuth even zoo een dier is als d'Elephant'.[18]

The distribution of mammoths' remains, and the concepts of the West Siberians, take on great significance when related to James's mention of the mammoth and the course of Russian expansion into Siberia. James wrote in 1618, so we can be sure that the word had entered the Russian language by then. However, in 1618 the Russian expansion into Siberia was far from complete. One language in which the source of the word has frequently been sought—Yakut—must be excluded, as the Russians did not reach Yakut territory until the 1620s. Similarly, Yukagir and Chukchi and the other East Siberian languages must be excluded as the immediate source of the word.

In 1618 Russian expansion had just reached the outer borders of Western Siberia, marked by the River Enisei. The first mention of the Enisei occurs in 1598, when 'енисейские соболи' are recorded.[19] Tribute was first exacted from Tungus families on the Enisei in 1607, and by 1614 eight families were paying tribute.[20] It was only in the 1620s and 1630s that the Tungus were brought fully under Russian administration, so although possible, it is unlikely that 'mammoth' has a Tungus etymology. Information travelled slowly from the borders of the Russian Empire to the interior; for example, although it was discovered in 1610 that the Enisei is navigable to the Arctic Ocean, the news did not reach Tobol'sk—let alone Moscow—until 1616.[21]

If the origin of 'mammoth' is to be sought in Siberia, then it must be sought in Western Siberia, among the Samoyeds, Ostyaks, Voguls, or possibly Kets or Tungus. James's location when he wrote his dictionary—Kholmogory—suggests that mammoth ivory was entering Russia by the northern route rather than by the southern route, control of which eventually led to the conquest of Siberia. The report that Jonas Logan brought back to England an 'elephant's tooth' from the land of the Samoyeds in 1611 confirms this,[22] and there may be another indirect indication in Descelier's

---

[17] B. Laufer, *Ivory in China* (Field Museum of Natural History: Anthropology, leaflet no. 25) (Chicago, 1925), 30–1.

[18] Ides, loc. cit. (n. 15).

[19] M. I. Belov, 'Pinezhskii letopisets o razvedochnom pokhode pomorov v Mangazeyu', in *Rukopisnoe nasledie drevnei Rusi* (L., 1972), 281.

[20] N. N. Stepanov, 'Prisoedinenie vostochnoi Sibiri v XVII v. i tungusskie plemena', in *Russkoe naselenie Pomor'ya i Sibiri: period feodalizma. Sbornik statei pamyati V. I. Shunkova* (M., 1973), 106–7.

[21] S. V. Bakhrushin, *Ocherki po istorii kolonizatsii Sibiri v XVI i XVII vv.* (M., 1927), 85.

[22] Laufer, op. cit. (n. 17), 31.

mappemonde of 1550 (Brit. Mus. Add. MS 24065), which in general locates palaearctic animals correctly, and accurately distinguishes African and Indian elephants, but depicts an elephant in Russia to the east of the White Sea.[23] If this is accepted as evidence for a Russian trade in mammoth ivory, then the trade must antedate even the conquest of Siberia in 1583, before which date the northern route was the only one available to Russia. Direct trade between the Samoyedic and Ugric peoples and the Russians makes a Tatar source for 'mammoth' unlikely.

The Muscovite trade route to Siberia before 1583 led north to the River Pechora, then across the Urals and down the Northern Sos'va to the Gulf of Ob'. Another route—the sea route—led from Kholmogory along the coast to the Yamal peninsula, and again to the Ob'. Between the Russians and the Samoyeds in European Russia are the Komi (Zyrian) people; they themselves have displaced the Ugric peoples, who in former times lived on both side of the Urals, but now only to the east of them. In the nineteenth century there were still some Vogul settlements to the west of the Urals, but whether these were a relict population or part of a minor re-migration from the east is uncertain. Early sources do not reliably distinguish Ostyaks and Voguls, but presuming no major unrecorded displacement has taken place, it seems likely that the Voguls have remained to the west of the Ostyaks in the course of their drift to the east. So even if Vogul tribes had not been encountered on the trade route on the upper reaches of the Pechora (the main area of Ugric settlement west of the Urals) they would be the first people to be encountered on the far side of the Urals, on the Northern Sos'va.

Extending from the Pechora to the Ob', the Voguls would be the first people the Muscovites met who lived surrounded by significant deposits of mammoth bones and tusks. The possible relevance for the etymology of *mammoth* of the Finno–Ugric words for 'earth', represented in Finnish by *maa*, in Ostyak by *mex*, in Vogul by *mā*, has already been pointed out by Räsänen,[24] but he dismisses it on the grounds that the second half of the word remains unexplained. As far as the Ugric branch is concerned the final *x* (in some dialects *γ*) in Ostyak is secondary, and the two languages share an original form of *m* + vowel. Vogul now has *ā* as the vowel, but some dialects preserve an earlier form in which the vowel is *ę* (middle-high unrounded back vowel). Steinitz cites Tavda dialect *mą̄*, Lower Konda *mâ*, Upper Loz'va and Sos'va *mā*, but Central and Upper Konda, Pelymka, Vagilsk and Central and Lower Loz'va *mę̄*.[25] The change *ę* > *a* is one of a series of vowel shifts which have taken place in Vogul since the fifteenth century (as changes undergone by Tatar loan-words show). This is in accordance with the earliest evidence we have for *mammoth*; the first known reference has *mai-* in the first syllable, which may be interpreted as [me], a Russification of [mę̄]; while Strahlenberg explicitly states that the change *me* > *ma* has taken place.

We have already remarked upon the lack of factual knowledge about the

[23] W. George, *Animals and Maps* (1969), 104, 126.
[24] Räsänen, op. cit. (n. 3), 293.
[25] W. Steinitz, *Geschichte des wogulischen Vokalismus* (Berlin, 1955), 187.

mammoth among the peoples of Siberia. An aspect of this is revealed by the words used to describe mammoths' tusks. James writes that 'they find his teeth or horns or bones in Pechore and Nova Zemla'. Bell of Antermony describes them as 'mammons' horns, so called by the natives'.[26] After describing the beliefs of various East Siberian peoples about the mammoth, Jochelson writes:

It is interesting to note that in the language of the above-mentioned tribes the mammoth ivory is called 'mammoth-horn' (e.g. the Yukaghir call it 'xólhut-ónmun', i.e. 'horn or antler of the mammoth') and not tusk or tooth, as if the people of today have no proper conception of the appearance of the mammoth. On the other hand, the natives know that the Siberian mammoth had a thick hairy tail and the 'horns' grew from the mouth.[27]

Although the second half of this statement cannot be applied to the natives of Western Siberia, the first half can. Modern designations for the mammoth relate it to horned or antlered animals: to the Samoyeds it can be the 'earth-bull', while the Voguls sometimes call it *mā-xar*, 'earth-stag'.[28]

The Vogul word for 'horn' is *oųtə*. The Ostyak form is *oŋət*, plural *oŋtət*. Vogul is the language which has innovated here, as cognate forms in Samoyed (e.g. Tavgi *ŋamta*) show. Thus Vogul has undergone the development *ŋt* > *ųt*. There is no indication of when the change took place. Nevertheless, Vogul provides us with phonological changes which are remarkably closely related to the various early forms recorded for *mammoth*.

The medial *m* must still be explained. Both Vogul and Ostyak do have *m* as a suffix forming, among other things, denominative nouns, often with no apparent difference in meaning from the original noun (e.g. Ostyak *xiśem* 'mould' <*xiśə*, idem; Vogul *ulm*, *ulêm* 'sleep', cf. Hungarian *álom*, idem <*ál* 'beneath').[29] The Vogul form *mām* is attested in the sense 'people' in a collection by Munkácsi.[30] The new meaning is obviously a secondary derivation from the basic meaning 'earth' and may be a later development than the formation of the noun *mām* itself.

Assuming a Vogul etymology, the word could develop in one of two ways:

$$*m\bar{e}moŋt\text{-} > *m\bar{a}moŋt\text{-} > *m\bar{a}moųt\text{-}$$
$$*m\bar{e}moŋt\text{-} > *m\bar{e}moųt\text{-} > *m\bar{a}moųt\text{-}$$

If both changes occurred more or less simultaneously, almost any of the forms could occur at a given time in different dialects, but to presume such dialectal diversity is unwarranted. The diversity of forms in European references suggests that possibly the word entered the Russian language while at an intermediate stage in Vogul; perhaps with a nasalized vowel in

[26] Bell, loc. cit. (n. 13).

[27] W. Jochelson, 'Some Notes on the Traditions of the Natives of North-East Siberia about the Mammoth', *American Naturalist*, xliii (1909), 49.

[28] Karjalainen, loc. cit. (n. 16).

[29] G. Sauer, *Die Nominalbildung im Ostjakischen* (Berlin, 1967), 27, and M. Kispál, *A vogul igenév mondattana* (Budapest, 1966), 197.

[30] B. Munkácsi, *Vogul népköltési gyüjtemény* (Budapest, 1892–1921), ii, 127 (twice). I am indebted to Mr. P. Sherwood, Lecturer in Hungarian at the School of Slavonic and East European Studies, London, for bringing this to my attention.

the second syllable (-*õt*). The dialectal coexistence of *mẹ̄* and *mā* is still attested today, so **mẹ̄mõt* and **māmõt* could have existed simultaneously. This assumption is not necessary to explain Strahlenberg's reference, as he is apparently aware of the change *mẹ̄ > mā*. In all probability the form became fixed as *mamont* in Russian only when large-scale Russian settlement took place in Siberia. The same Russian settlement would also influence the Vogul conception of the mammoth. *If mamont* is indeed 'earth-horn', then mammoth ivory was apparently not associated in the Vogul mind with any beast, real or mythical. Only Russian identification of mammoth ivory as a form of elephant tusk would make it necessary to identify 'earth-horn' with a real or imagined animal.

Regionalisms, German Loan-words, and Europeanisms in the Language of Jakub Bart-Ćišinski

By GERALD STONE

OUR ability to put the language of Ćišinski's literary works in its historic setting and to assess and characterize his role in the development of the Upper Sorbian literary language is inevitably limited by the extent to which we are able to draw on existing descriptions and histories of relevant aspects of both the literary language and non-standard varieties. Apart from studies of the evolution of the literary language[1] we would need, ideally, to be able to refer to descriptions of regional, social, and functional varieties of Sorbian. The question of style is especially important. Regional variation has received, and continues to receive, the attention of dialectologists,[2] but social and functional variation, and stylistics have been neglected or ignored. It is consequently quite possible to identify a number of regional features in Ćišinski's language without being any the wiser as to their aesthetic function. Similarly, it is a relatively simple matter to identify the German loan-words and Europeanisms[3] in his language, but their motivation frequently remains obscure.

This article is based on a reading of a mere handful of Ćišinski's works, and any conclusions must therefore be regarded as provisional and subject to possible revision in the light of subsequent examination of a larger corpus. The objective is to investigate the poet's use of regionalisms (i.e. elements from his native dialect), of German loan-words, and of Europeanisms. In one or two cases tentative observations on their stylistic implications are included.

In view of the special position of the Sorbian language in society,

---

[1] E.g. J. Páta, 'Spisovný jazyk lužickosrbský' in *Slovanské spisovné jazyky v době přítomné*, ed. M. Weingart (Prague, 1937), 107–20, and H. Schuster-Šewc, 'Die Geschichte der sorbischen Schriftsprachen (ein Grundriß)' in *Slavyanska filologiya*, iii (Sofia, 1963),135–51.

[2] The *Sorbischer Sprachatlas* being produced by the linguistic section of the Sorbian Ethnological Institute in Bautzen is gradually facilitating the study of certain aspects of the standard languages. Five volumes (i–iv and xi) have been published so far (1965, 1968, 1970, 1972, 1975).

[3] On German loan-words see H. H. Bielfeldt, *Die deutschen Lehnwörter im Obersorbischen* (Leipzig, 1933). By the term 'Europeanism' I understand a borrowing whose immediate source cannot be identified owing to the fact that possible sources exist in a number of European languages. The concept is admittedly problematic. See my 'Lexical Changes in the Upper Sorbian Literary Language during and following the National Awakening', *Lětopis Instituta za serbski ludospyt*, series A, xviii (1971), 4–8, and A. Šivic–Dular's review of the latter in *Slavistična revija*, xxii (1974), 243–4.

particularly its position *vis-à-vis* German, it may be useful to refer briefly
and in general terms to the question of the social and functional distribution
of these two languages in Ćišinski's time and earlier. Until the mid nineteenth
century the prestige language in Lusatia was German. It was the language of
the ruling class, the language of power and control. Sorbian, on the other
hand, was the language of the peasantry, for nearly all Sorbs were peasants.
So homogeneous was the Sorbian population that one might almost say that
Sorbian and German were socially in complementary distribution. In the
interests of strict accuracy, however, their distribution must be described as
overlapping, though the overlap was clearly of insignificant proportions.
Anyone who rose above the status of peasant would have to adopt German
as his first language. As to such anomalous groups as the clergy, it is probable
that, whatever a man's origin, he always clearly belonged to one class or
the other. The clergy in fact, including those of Sorbian origin, belonged to
the German-speaking class, but most of them, including many of German
origin, used Sorbian as a second language for certain purposes. So far as
Sorbian was concerned, the question of social dialects did not arise: there
was no such thing as 'U' and 'non-U' in Upper Sorbian before about 1840.
German was 'U'; Sorbian was 'non-U'.[4]

There were, however, functionally differentiated varieties of Sorbian. Without going into this matter too deeply, it is surely clear that there was at least
one distinct register—that in use in church services. And the use of this
register was probably extended to certain other solemn occasions. But there
were also certain situations in which change of register meant change of
language. In dealings with the authorities, for example, it was appropriate
to use German, and we need not doubt that on certain occasions, particularly
in towns, those few Sorbs who knew German would speak it even to each
other.[5] Moreover, German was often used instead of Sorbian in the Church,
if, for example, the pastor knew no Sorbian. In the Church therefore a certain
register of German and the Sorbian register of solemnity were distribution-
ally equivalent. It is thus likely that this Sorbian register was particularly
prone to German interference, especially as the clergy probably constituted
the only social group in which Sorbian and German were in close contact.
The register of solemnity was characterized by the presence of certain German elements. The language of the 1728 Bible, in particular, for all the
translators' protestations of 'purity',[6] is probably more affected by German
interference than the spoken language was at that time. This applies particularly to the frequent use of the articles, which may well have given

---

[4] On the categories 'U' (upper class) and 'Non-U' see A. S. C. Ross, 'Linguistic Class-
Indicators in Present-Day English', *Neuphilologische Mitteilungen*, lv (Helsinki, 1954), 20–56.
[5] An article in *Tydźenska Nowina* for 13 September 1845 (no. 38) asked: 'Štó njewě, zo
hewak Serbja z wušich stawow, hdyž hromadu přindźechu, jenož němski rěčachu?' ('Who
does not know that otherwise Sorbs of the higher classes, whenever they came together,
would speak only German?')
[6] *Biblia, to je zyłe Szwjate Pißmo stareho a noweho Zakona . . . wot njekotrych Evangeliskich
Prjedarjow pschełożena* (Bautzen, 1728). The translators in their foreword inform the reader
that he will find here a 'correct and pure Sorbian language', and state that they have taken
pains to avoid the use of foreign words.

Sorbian peasants reading the Bible (or hearing it read) an impression of sublime solemnity.[7]

Evidence of the high status of Germanisms in spoken Sorbian, even in the second half of the nineteenth century, is given in a prefatory remark by Jan Radyserb-Wjela to a list of lexical Germanisms collected by him:[8]

Za nje ma naša rěč z wjetša swoje narodne słowa, kotrež pak zdźěla z njerodu so njewužiwaju a zdźěla wulcyčinjenja dla. ('Instead of them our language has in most cases its own native words, which however are not used, partly from carelessness and partly in order to show off.')

But though Sorbian peasants might still regard the use of German loan-words as a way of showing off, the attitudes of the newly developed Sorbian bourgeoisie and intelligentsia were evolving in the opposite direction. After 1840 the endeavours of intellectuals to rid the literary language of Germanisms and introduce loans of various kinds from other Slavonic languages led to changes in its stylistic stratification. Among users of the new literary language German loan-words were no longer of high status and many of them were virtually excluded from literary use altogether.

It is consequently scarcely surprising that the publication in 1878 of Ćišinski's article 'Hłosy ze Serbow do Serbow'[9] caused something of a stir in literary circles. In it he castigated the kind of nationalistic purism which had by now established its own tradition of intolerance, because, as he claimed, it was causing the literary language to grow away from the vernacular and to become the property of a privileged few—the intelligentsia.[10] He agreed that it was the business of grammarians to order and stabilize what he called the 'formal element' of the language, but saw the German loan-words in Sorbian as an inevitable result of contact with the German language which could not be altered.[11]

The use of the written language for secular purposes was a new development in the nineteenth century; the system of styles and registers was therefore still unstable. But purism was tending to allocate the German loan-words collectively to a particular place in the system, even though most Sorbs in Ćišinski's time were not particularly aware of the German origin of many of them.[12]

In view of Ćišinski's rejection of purism the position of Germanisms in his own usage is obviously a matter of some importance, but before considering this, I should like to mention briefly his use of regionalisms and his position

[7] This idea arises from a conversation with Dr. Frido Michałk.
[8] 'Cuze słowa we serbskej rěči, kiž abo w serbskim słowniku steja abo so často mjez ludom słyša, hačrunje serbskeho pochada njejsu', a manuscript in the remains of the Maćica Serbska's archives now housed among the Sorbian Central Archives in the Sorbian Ethnological Institute at Bautzen (ref. XLIX/7 A). It bears no date but belongs to the second half of the nineteenth century. I am obliged to the Institute's director Professor Pawoł Nowotny and to its archivist Dr. Frido Mětšk for allowing me access to the manuscript during a visit to Bautzen in 1965.
[9] Lipa Serbska (July 1878), 80–4.
[10] Ibid. 83.
[11] Ibid.
[12] '. . . su . . . přetworjene, zo je my hižo ani hako němske nječujemy' ('. . . are . . . transformed so that we no longer even feel them to be German') (ibid. 84).

vis-à-vis the supra-dialectal norm. He was born and brought up in Kukow (Kukau), one of the Catholic villages to the west and north-west of Bautzen, and he was a Catholic priest. Quite naturally, however, he wrote in the secular literary language of his time, which had been adapted for secular purposes from the language of Protestant writings based on the Bautzen dialect. Catholics had once had their own literary language, based on the dialect of the Catholic villages, but by the time Ćišinski appeared on the literary scene considerable progress towards unification of Catholic and Protestant variants had been made, largely as a result of the work of Michał Hórnik. *Lipa Serbska*, the journal in which 'Hłosy ze Serbow do Serbow' was published, was non-sectarian; it published contributions on secular subjects from both Protestants and Catholics. Nevertheless, it is often possible to detect the local (and therefore religious) origins of these authors from local features in their language.

In 'Hłosy ze Serbow do Serbow' Ćišinski in nearly all cases uses the Protestant (Bautzen) morpheme *-eho* for the genitive singular of masculine and neuter adjectives: e.g. '. . . serbskeho luda . . .' (ibid. 80), '. . . myslički mjenowaneho spisa . . .' (ibid. 83).[13] He uses the same morpheme in pronouns too: e.g. '. . . so kaž klěšć teho dźerži, čehož je sej za młode nadobył . . .' (ibid. 80), '. . . wot njeho . . .' (ibid. 84). In two places in this essay, however, the Catholic variant *-oho* appears, viz. '. . . ryč je kubło a wobsedźeństwo cyłoho ludu . . .' (ibid. 83), and '. . . stejišćo swojoho ludu . . .' (ibid.). The abbreviated genitive in *-oh* (feminine in *-ej*) is also well represented here. The masculine and neuter dative singular adjectives and pronouns nearly all have the Protestant ending *-emu*, but we also find '. . . přećiwo přewulkom purismej . . .' (ibid. 84) and '. . . k ničom . . .' (ibid. 83).

Another characteristically Catholic feature occurring in the essay (but only once) is the morpheme *-njo* (for Protestant standard *-nje*) in neuter verbal nouns, viz. '. . . na přistojne a přimerjene wašnjo . . .' (ibid. 80). Further on, however, the variant *wašnje* occurs (83).

Catholic forms are also encountered occasionally in Ćišinski's poetry: e.g. *toho* (for Protestant standard *teho*) in 'Ćerpjacy młodźenc' (translated from Petrarch, *Kniha sonettow*, 61),[14] in one of the poems from the cycle 'W zymnicy' (*Ze žiwjenja*, 67),[15] and in 'Miłoćičanska žaba' (*Za ćichim*, 128, 130);[16] *wšoho* (Protestant standard *wšeho*) in 'Bohabojosć' (*Za ćichim*, 61); *tomu* (Protestant standard *temu*) in 'Pólskej' (translated from Kollár, *Kniha sonettow*, 66), and in the introductory poem 'Zawod' to the cycle 'W zymnicy' (*Ze žiwjenja*, 60); *čomu* (Protestant standard *čemu*) in 'Keklija swěta' (*Ze žiwjenja*, 39), and in 'Z wonka—z nutřka' (*Za ćichim*, 68). In fact, so far as these pronouns (*tón, wšón, što*) are concerned, the Catholic forms predominate in Ćišinski's poetry.[17] But all other pronouns and all adjectives

---

[13] In view of the possible significance of orthographic subtleties all quotations from the works of Ćišinski are given in the original spelling.

[14] *Kniha sonettow* (Bautzen, 1884).

[15] *Ze žiwjenja* (Bautzen, 1899).

[16] *Za ćichim* (Bautzen, 1906).

[17] As examples of the Protestant variants we may mention *čemu* and *wšemu* in *Kniha sonettow* (56 and 66 respectively).

in the poems examined have either the Protestant morphemes *-eho*, *-emu*, or abbreviated types such as *jom'* (*Ze žiwjenja*, 59, 94), *druhoh'* (*Za ćichim*, 127). Full Catholic forms in *-oho*, *-omu*, do not occur. It must be admitted, of course, that one of the imponderables in the study of these texts is the extent to which they have been edited.

In view of the fact that Pfuhl describes *joho*, *njoho* (*joh*, *njoh*) and *jomu*, *njomu* (*jom*, *njom*) as 'Vulgärformen', and refers to *toho*, *tomu* (*toh*, *tom*) and the adjectival endings *-oho*, *-omu* as 'Nebenformen, die sich für die edlere Sprache nicht eignen',[18] one might expect them, when used in literature, to be stylistically marked. However, I have found no evidence of this in the works of Ćišinski.

Apart from the pronominal variants already mentioned, Catholic features are relatively rare in Ćišinski's poetry. The protestant form *ranje* occurs in *Kniha sonettow* (6, 18) and in *Ze žiwjenja* (3), but in *Swětło z wyšiny*[19] (56) we find the Catholic variant *ranjo*. He consistently distinguishes between *-li* and *-łe* forms in the perfect tense (a distinction unknown to the Catholic dialect). The standard *fijałka* 'violet' occurs quite often, but not one instance has been found of *fijonka*, the form used in Ćišinski's native region.[20] It is sometimes clear, however, that the word *hordy* in his usage is to be understood as having its Catholic meaning 'splendid', 'magnificent', rather than the Protestant meaning 'proud', and it is significant that he translates the title of his poem 'Sic transit gloria mundi' as 'Tak hordosć swěta zakhadźa'.[21]

Turning to the question of Ćišinski's use of Germanisms, it may be said straight away that he did follow his own anti-puristic principle, and did not shrink from using several German loan-words disapproved of by others. This may be seen from the following examples:

FAKLA 'torch': 'Hlej, z dala hižo swěća fakle!' ('Glossa', *Ze žiwjenja*, 38). (This word was not included in any of the Upper Sorbian dictionaries published in the nineteenth and early twentieth centuries.)

LÓFT 'air': 'A njewisa naša pisomna ryč čisće w lófće?' ('Hłosy ze Serbow do Serbow', 83). (The tendency was for *lóft* to be replaced by *powětr/powětro*. Ćišinski used the latter in *Swětło z wyšiny*, 94.)

MEWA 'sea-gull': 'Mevam pěseń zynči do pokoja' ('Mórske błyšćenje' from the cycle 'Na sewjernym morju', *Ze žiwjenja*, 11); 'Mevy k wam so k starym znatym kłonja . . .' ('Pohrjebnišćo bjezmjencow', from the same cycle, ibid. 23). (This word was given in none of the nineteenth-century and early twentieth-century dictionaries. I have yet to find it in use in the works of any other writer.)

RYCHTOWAĆ 'to direct': '. . . njedostatki tychsamych rozjasnić a na lěpše rychtować' ('Hłosy ze Serbow do Serbow', 80).

SORTA 'sort': 'Za złotom njedrapa, kaž słaba sorta/Tych, kotřiž za mjaso, za proch so pala' ('Jasny duch a časny wuspěch', *Za ćichim*, 55); 'Psy

---

[18] Ch. Tr. Pfuhl, *Laut- und Formenlehre der oberlausitzisch-wendischen Sprache* (Bautzen, 1867), 64, 66.

[19] Published posthumously, Bautzen, 1911.

[20] See H. Faßke, H. Jentsch, S. Michalk, *Sorbischer Sprachatlas*, iii (Bautzen, 1970), 275.

[21] J. Ćišinski, 'Z křidłom worjołskim', *Časopis Maćicy Serbskeje*, 1903, p. 103. In *Nowa Doba*, 15 Jan. 1972, p. 3, the same Latin phrase is translated with 'słava'.

kołowokoł' čušla dźiwnej' sorty/ A wopuš bojaznje mjez nohi kładu;'
('Sequere me!', *Swětło z wyšiny*, 44). (This word was extremely rare in literature. It was not included in any of the dictionaries published during the
nineteenth and early twentieth centuries.)

The question now arises whether the German loan-words in Ćišinski's
works can be allotted to a particular stylistic stratum. Before the Sorbian
national awakening German loan-words were probably neutral stylistically
in most cases, though (as indicated above) some of them may have been
marked as literary or formal. In the new literary language Germanisms
tended to be omitted altogether, but since they continued to be used in
colloquial speech they constituted a potential source of marked forms which
could have been used for special effect in literature, either detracting in some
way from the referent or possibly with some other particular connotation.
Ćišinski made use of this source. His use of *sorta* in the locations cited is for
colloquial and slightly pejorative effect. The literary word *družina* would
have been less expressive here. Similarly, the loan-word *mewa* is used for
special effect. It is even spelt with a -*v*- in order to draw attention to itself.
(Whether this spelling was intended to suggest a particular pronunciation
is another question.) Any of the literary words for 'sea-gull' (*rybornak*,
rybačka, *tonuška*) would have been stylistically neutral or literary.

Ćišinski's use of *mewa* and *sorta* (and probably of other Germanisms too)
must have surprised his readers. But surely the feature of his language most
shocking to his contemporaries must have been his use of Europeanisms.
Their effect is most striking when they are used in close proximity to each
other. The following extracts from his poems may serve as examples:

> 'Do theatrow, na koncerty khodźić,
> Móda wosebneho swěta je.'
>> ('Keklija swěta', *Ze žiwjenja*, 39)

> 'Błysk ducha, słowow raz a myslow skalnosć
> So diskredituje za njenormalnosć.'
>> ('Kak so čini', *Za ćichim*, 66)

> 'Na jewišću jako w tragoediji
> Rjekowje do boja stupaju!
> A pak jako w błudnej komoediji
> Pojacy so z tryskom tołkaju.'
>> ('Ego sum via . . .', *Swětło z wyšiny*, 40)

It is fairly clear that in each of these three extracts the Europeanisms have a
particular connotative function.

In Ćišinski's prose, on the other hand, the Europeanisms were apparently
intended to be stylistically neutral. But it is ironic that in the very work in
which he complained of the discrepancy between the literary language and
everyday language he should use phrases like: 'Tute rozestajenja njeńdźa
pak nihdy hole theoretiske abstrakcije subjektivneho myslenja jenotliwcow
. . .' ('Hłosy ze Serbow do Serbow', 80), and '. . . štóž chce princip, tón
dyrbi tež konsequency z principa sćěhowace nolens volens chcyć a zamołwjeć'
(ibid. 84). It is doubtful whether the less well educated sections of the Sorbian
public found this kind of language any easier to understand than the puristic

language which Ćišinski was attacking. At the same time, his use of certain other Europeanisms[22] in place of their puristic synonyms quite clearly did tend to make his language more accessible to ordinary people: e.g. *echo* (instead of *wothłós*), *komedija* (instead of *wjeselohra*), *mašina* (instead of *strój* or *nastroj*), *teatr* (instead of *dźiwadło*), *tragedija* (instead of *struchłohra*). On the other hand, lacking the bigotry of some purists, he did not disdain to use the Slavonic neologisms on occasion. Many of them after all were well established in the literary vocabulary before Ćišinski appeared on the scene. The outstanding innovatory characteristic of his vocabulary, however, is his widespread use of Europeanisms in poetry.

[22] There is sometimes room for argument as to whether a given word is best regarded as a Europeanism or as a German loan-word.